FOOD FOR THOUGHT

Written and Illustrated by:
Kirsten J. Cunha

Cover Art by: Kathryn Keene

For Mom.

For Dad.

For Connor.

For Kylie.

For Wendy.

For Fr. Rich.

I would like to share with you a very personal, authentic glimpse into what occurs in the mind of someone undergoing recovery for an eating disorder: from the day of admission to the day of discharge.

If you, or someone you know, is struggling with an eating disorder, please seek help. Do not wait until it is too late. You can always contact the National Eating Disorder Association Helpline at 1-800-931-2237, or visit NationalEatingDisorders.org for more information.

It is never too late to help yourself, or someone else.

PREFACE

Self-compassion, loving yourself, and loving your body, are perhaps the aims of recovery, which require the most strenuous effort to achieve. The ability to acknowledge one's sufferings can be daunting. It can feel weakening. With no help from profiting media, it is so easy to hide behind the mask of social platforms. We can "filter" the imperfections of our reality. Social media allows us to portray the "highlight reel" of our lives—to celebrate life's most beautiful moments; to reminisce on our "highs"—to paint a portrait of a life we could only imagine. While these moments have their place, it can lead one to believe that the opposite moments simply don't exist in the lives of others. Sadness isn't as glamorous as happiness.

This book is for those who feel alone in their struggles. This is for those who are fighting to bear their cross. This is for anyone who has fought to the point of remission and recovery, and for those who fight the battle to stay healthy every day. This is for anyone who has found him, or herself, in relapse. This is for those who desire education on the inner dialogue that has plagued one ED survivor. This is for those who crave insight. This is for anyone who needs validation that he/she is not alone. We are warriors.

Remember that you have the power to overcome. I know you do. You have a beautiful light inside of you—we are all born with an inner motivation. It is unlike any other. It is like a flame. Harness it. Ignite it. Allow it to rage like a wildfire. Regardless of who you are, or what you have done, you deserve recovery. You deserve happiness.

So, yes, you *can* do it. While your demons may dissipate all essence of hope and joy in your life, I promise that you still have a choice. You can choose **life**. Remember who you were before the illness, the condition, the malice, the eating disorder, etc. took hold. Find that being inside of you—the one who is healthy, happy, resilient, and who loves himself/herself. It may not seem like it, but they are there. All of the time you've spent at war with yourself has not destroyed them, but has simply silenced them. Let them scream. Let them shout. Allow yourself to finally be heard. There is a light. There is hope.

And if you ever find yourself without purpose to keep going, let me just tell you...

...Happiness looks beautiful on you.

DECEMBER

THE BEGINNING

December 6
Day 1

What would my life be like if I didn't care about what other people thought?

       Well, if I didn't care about what other people thought, I wouldn't be here. Today was my intake day at The Flourish Collaborative. I had a final this morning in Upper Extremity Practicum. As stressful as it was, it really helped to distract me from this whole situation. I spent my morning thinking of differential diagnoses, instead of dreaming about the lunch of three broccoli florets that I packed. To be honest, anything that didn't revolve around food was a distraction deserving of an Oscar. During that painful ninety minute exam, I scoured my brain. I aimed to recall any information from those past four months. I tried to dismiss the intrusive thoughts of my twelve-year-old boyish physique and overall hideousness. I agonized over the fact that I couldn't focus on anything for more than eight seconds. I wondered if medial epicondylitis was exacerbated by wrist flexion, or by wrist extension. I prayed that my classmates didn't think that I looked fat today.

       The semester was not one for the books, to say the least. I've been battling an eating disorder. I started dieting and exercising as a way to cope with the stresses of daily college life. I got a new job. Classes got tougher. I lost touch with a few friends. I felt alone.

       When things in your life seem to come at you like unwavering bullets, I found it comforting to look towards those things I *could* monitor and *could* stabilize. I considered picking up a hobby, like maybe painting or reading. However, when yearning for structure, you come to find value in only the quantifiable. So, needless to say, neither Monet nor Jane Austen did it for me. That was when I found exercise. You see, it was so easy to track the calories burnt, or the distances traveled. I then realized that it was just as simple to calculate the calories you intake each day. You could set a goal. When all else seems to go crumby, a calorie deficit was the one thing I could always achieve. That's when things quickly spiraled out of control. Restricting myself became a defense mechanism against any challenge that came my way.

I got by for the first few months. My friends and family initially thought I was an "inspiration" for finally getting into shape. Left and right, my peers were asking me for advice. My own doctor asked me for my "secret". It wasn't until I dropped the last of my sixty pounds that the idolizing stares turned into looks of disgust and fear. It wasn't until then that my physician dismissed me with: "You're going to die", as opposed to "You're going to have a great semester!"

I can't even look at myself in the mirror. My skin is broken out, my hair resembles straw, and my butt is a literal pancake. I used to think that I'd catch people staring at me because they thought I was beautiful. Now, I feel as though, all along, it's because they are afraid of me.

The day was dull, cloudy, and grey—kind of like my personality has been over the last few months. Once I got out of class, I sprinted to my car. I prayed that those few active minutes could've burned off my breakfast. I had a psychiatrist appointment in Westport in twenty minutes. After that, it was finally time to begin my new adventure—recovery.

Dr. Andrew's office always provided me with a sense of homeyness. The decor was eclectic. Her office sat on the top floor of this rustic brick building. The interior resembled that of a 1950s hotel, coupled with a T.G.I. Friday's. The carpets were red velvet, and the wallpaper was as gold as a Klimt painting. There was a poster on the wall that read:

> *Everyone is a genius. But if you judge a fish by its ability to climb a tree, it will live its whole life believing that it is stupid.*

I thought that was nice. I mean, in a "you should probably feel better about yourself" kind of way. It's appropriate.

The doctor was seeing another client, so I had some alone time with my thoughts. I thought about the day. It was Tuesday, or maybe Wednesday. Things have become sort of blurry over the last few months. I wondered if Dr. Andrew would think that I got fatter since our last appointment.

My inner dialogue was interrupted when she arose from her office. She wore a smile that was genuine, but way too big for her line of work. After a lengthy conversation about my concerns towards beginning intensive therapy, she assured me that the place was "grand". "Kirsten," she said, "if any of my children were inflicted with an eating disorder. I mean, God-forbid should that ever happen... TFC is where I'd send them in a heartbeat."

Ugh.

The term "eating disorder" never sat well with me. I find it cringe-worthy, as if someone whispered a word like "moist" into my ear. Yuck. I prefer "eating issue" or "personal problem". I mean, c'mon. I'm twenty years old. I'm an adult. The three things I need to do in order to simply live are to breathe, to sleep, and to eat. I can't even do one of those things properly. How embarrassing is that? It just further perpetuates the fact that I'm a failure.

The appointment made me anxious, and, afterward, I began my drive down the Merritt Parkway. In anticipation, I imagined the best-case scenario: my bony knees curled up on a comfy couch, surrounded by lots of pretty and fluffy pillows. I imagined parking in the driveway of a gorgeous mansion, resting on the hills of the Greenwich, Connecticut countryside. Someone told me once that Judge Judy lived in Greenwich. Maybe she'd be friends with my counselor. Maybe she'd live next door, and I'd get to see her watering the flowers, or getting the mail, or doing activities that normal people do instead of calorie counting.

Ha. Wasn't that a dream. When I arrived, I was starstruck at what I saw before me. After getting off of the exit, I circled the same desolate street about four times before realizing that my GPS wasn't lying to me. TFC was located in a sketchy little office building, sort of reminiscent of Dunder Mifflin. I swallowed my pride as I parked my little white Sonata in the cobblestone driveway. How bad could it be?

Note to self: Never ask yourself 'how bad could it be'. Never. Because I can tell you with the utmost certainty, that if you have to ask yourself that, odds are, it will be a lot worse than you could prepare yourself for.

I made my way up to the third floor of the building. As my eyes met the elevator, and without a second thought, I pivoted my body straight towards the stairs. Once I reached the top of the mountain of steps, I ran into the bathroom. The climb had embarrassingly winded me. I needed to take a break to regroup. "Still," I thought, "I don't need this place".

Inside, the walls were so hauntingly white that I could have sworn that they whispered for a pumpkin spiced latte with extra foam. My mom was sitting on a bench next to the elevator. She drove here from work to make sure I turned up for my intake. Smart woman.

The first person we met was MaryLou. She's the secretary, I think. She was an absolute sweetheart, who was trying a little too hard not to hurt my feelings. MaryLou's office was in the back of the paper-supply-company. She guided me to her back room, where, together, we filled out the paperwork. My mom sat uncomfortably in the corner of the office, as I unwillingly skimmed the countless consent forms and surveys. My mother twiddled her thumbs, and, in those mere forty-five minutes, the anxiety she carried had aged her. Signing all of these documents made me feel as though I was signing my life away. Or, like I was selling my soul. I mean, it could go either way, right? I could be leasing my spirit to this community home. With some time, I may be able to trade in my worn down being for a new model.

I found myself fidgeting in MaryLou's office. The furniture reminded me of the old Queen's Village tag sales that my grandma and I used to drive past. I anxiously played with my necklace and traced the chain around to the clasp, where a huge knot kept it around my neck. I always told myself that once I got the knot out, I would give the chain to my sister. I wondered if I'd ever be able to release myself from its grasp. I wondered if the shackles that bound me to this life would ever give way.

Anyway, MaryLou awoke me from my trance and led me towards the office of my new therapist. Her name was Rebecca, I think, or maybe Diane? She was okay. She had a princess tiara, and a bunch of bunny rabbit photos, pinned to her bulletin board. "She must be absolutely insane," I thought, "or maybe she's just a royal bunny breeder". Also, she was only wearing foundation with no eye makeup, which made her look like a zombie—ready to eat all of our emaciated brains.

I met the dietician next. Her name was Elizabeth, and meeting her was like a breath of fresh air. She was such a ray of sunshine, and I imagine that she would've played Ms. Potts or Mother Goose in a Young Thespians group. She inquired about my food rituals, and about the fears that had become so second nature to me. When she and I concluded our talk, I met my mom in the family group room, where the rest of the clients were gathered.

I was surprised by the eyes I met as I scanned the room. You see, our struggles have a way of turning us a little egocentric. Through the entirety of this battle, I always thought I was the only one struggling. I thought that I was the only one who hated the chamber of her soul. I thought that I was the only one who could never see anything but imperfections and shame. Yet, as I entered the room, the 'L' shaped couch was stuffed with families, and children, and other miscellaneous loved ones. They sat shoulder to shoulder, as if smothered in a container like a bunch of sardines. My mother sat in the middle of the room. Her arms were woven across her body, as if shielding her ribs from the horrors that escaped these young warrior's mouths.

As I made my way across the room, hopping and leaping over tear-filled tissues and folded legs, I met my mom on the couch. The looks that I received, from the other girls in the room, could have literally killed. It was funny, I thought. The only way I could describe those stares is, in a sense, similar to the way that my eating disorder forces me to view myself. This is going to be an interesting adventure.

December 7

Day 2

Dinner on Wednesday was…

Well… it could have gone a lot better.

Wednesday was restaurant night. In the group before our restaurant outing, we spoke about ways in which we *don't* practice self-care. I was pretty embarrassed to see that I spend the majority of my existence practicing negative boundary behaviors, as opposed to positive ones.

Before I went home yesterday, Elizabeth requested to meet with me again. She had forgotten to give me my meal plan. I really liked the plan she formulated. I felt like it was super realistic and attainable. I was provided with a certain amount of carbohydrates, proteins, and fats to complete at each meal. The plan was much smaller than ones that other outpatient dieticians had requested I follow. Elizabeth told me that she wanted to see what I could do before she threw any major challenges at me.

Finally, someone is extending an olive branch. I was hit by a wave of motivation and confidence. That confidence carried me through today. Well, that was until I remembered that we soon would have to take our restaurant orders. Anxiety filled my being. Imagine being in the center of the Roman Colosseum. People are chanting all around you. They're screaming and cheering in anticipation of your ultimate demise. You're paralyzed. You're waiting for the ravenous bull to approach behind the gates, and be released. You are unable to control the timing. You cannot say anything. You cannot do anything.

You cannot feel anything. You are trapped. That's what it's like.

On my drive to The Flourish Collaborative, I had a pep-talk with myself. "You can do anything you set your mind to" I thought. "Italian food? Mexican food? You got this!" However, there was one genre of food I knew would give me a run for my money. Chinese food. And guess what menu was handed to me in Elizabeth's little sanctuary of an office?

Chinese.

My life is a joke. It's an actual joke. I decided that I was going to make a really big effort on my first day, so I ordered Lo Mein. Oh my gosh, what was I thinking? When I was handed the menu, my eyes darted back in forth in panic. Where were the calorie counts? Where were the symbols that highlighted the more health-conscious items? I immediately regretted my request of the oil-drenched noodles, until I instantly became flooded with flashbacks.

Suddenly, I was no longer in the less-than-ideal office building. I was sitting in Chinatown with my grandma, as we had done so many times in the past. I remembered how we would relive those memories by ordering Chinese takeout to her musty Queens Village living room. My eyes would glance back and forth from *Jeopardy* to the lavish painting of dead-sunflowers, which hung high above the couch. How I wish I could just go back there, to those times with the cigarette-stained carpet. Instead, I'm here. I'm surrounded by tear-stained shaggy rugs, and fear.

December 8
Day 3

Life is not a supplement.
      You can choose to live life,
      or you can choose
      To substitute it with "fillers".
      Do you want life?
      Or, do you want
      To choose a supplement?

      Also, *Ensure* tastes like actual gasoline, so you can use that as motivation.

December 9
Day 4

Dear Body,

Thank you for pumping my veins with blood—
nutrient-rich and zestful for opportunity. Thank you for
hearing all sounds—both pleasant and not. Be it the
basketball alarm, my growling stomach, or the sweet song
of the feathered friends that wake me up each morning. I
am grateful to take in every last pitch. My body, you
remind me to never go a second without taking in all of
life's experiences. Thank you for allowing me to smell.
Thank you for allowing me to see. Thank you for
allowing me to experience so much more than the
materialistic side of this world.

But, oh my body. My dear psyche.

How dare you.
How dare you set me on this track.
How dare you restrict me
Of my craving for life.

December 10
Day 5

Adapt.

The thoughts that invaded your mind
Roared like thunder.
You felt your faults rain on you
Like droplets.
They fell like
Metal coins
From the sky.

This rain flooded your Earth.
You tried to swim.
You searched and searched
For your Noah and his arc.
Still, the waves regressed you.

You ask the world:
"Where am I supposed to go?
When there's no more sun to light the path,
What am I supposed to do?"
And then the world answered you:
"Where do ducks go after fall?"

December 11
Day 6

Things I Am Grateful for:

1. The little ice cream shop outside of Caernarfon Castle. They have raspberry sorbet and cute employees.
2. TED talks.
3. Those friends that may not know what is wrong right away, but do not walk away. Instead, they reach out their hand.
4. My dog's toothy smile.
5. Finishing that essay before it's due.
6. Movie theaters that have the fancy CocaCola machines.
7. Not following my meal plan.

December 12
Day 7

MaryLou took my vitals when I arrived at the Collaborative today.
She had me lie down on the velvet loveseat, which sat in the milieu. For ten minutes, I laid there in silence. This was my first time being weighed since my intake. I mean, I still weigh myself each day, but, I've been working on it! Now, I'll only weigh myself between seven or eight times, as opposed to ten—maybe twelve. Even though I know my weight, I felt my skin crawl over the judgemental eyes that would plague me when MaryLou saw the digits. I tried to do a breathing exercise to ease my anxiety, but was rudely interrupted by thoughts on how absolutely freaking ridiculous this is.

December 13
Day 8

Ignorance is not bliss.

Ignorance is the bad taste in your mouth. Ignorance is the empty pit in your stomach that not even the most delicious slice of hope can fill. I used to think that there was so much beauty in people completely ignoring what was going on with me. I mean, it helped my disordered thoughts cultivate more evidence that I was too fat, or not good enough, or not pretty enough, or not worthy of love. Now, I think ignorance is toxic. At the end of the day, doesn't everyone just want some validation? Some recognition that life sucks sometimes? Recognition that, in spite it all, they are doing the best that they can? Recognition that, even though there are 7 billion complete strangers around them, that they are truly not alone in their struggles? I don't know if that makes sense. I guess I just feel alone.

December 14
Day 9

I am lost at sea on a stormy night.
>   Or maybe it was a stormy week.
>   Or month.
>   Or year.
>   All of this time has turned dark and gray,
>   But mostly dark.
>   All I seem to remember
>   Are the echoes of self-hatred,
>   Or the numbers ingested,
>   Or the fear and isolation.

>   In spite of it all,
>   I found a glimmer of light
>   Leading me to land.

>   If I row hard enough,
>   Maybe I can make it.

December 15
Day 10

It's Day 10. Morale is low. Rage is high. Angst is real. Sass is at a whole other level.

Want to hear something funny? TFC doesn't have a nutritionist anymore. Should I be scared? Or maybe a little excited? No one is around anymore to monitor me. But, yeah. Elizabeth moved to Providence to do something with someone, or something like that.

The councilors just told us about it, and all of the clients gathered together in one of the group rooms. With tear-filled eyes, Elizabeth sat on an ottoman in the center of the room. One by one, each client went around the room and gave her an obituary.

They called these groups "Graduations". Apparently, they do it for all of the clients when they are discharged from treatment. It made me a little uncomfortable. Hearing all of the endearing words made me a little more depressed, as compared to any other emotion I was supposed to be feeling. I knew that I've never influenced anyone in the same way Elizabeth has touched the lives of these other clients.

I had so much planned for my life. I was going to change the world. Yet, here I am. All I'm good for is my ability to tell you the macronutrients of a single almond, or the number of steps I can track from my apartment door to the bus stop.

I was too invested in the thoughts of how large my thighs looked today to pay attention. So, anyway, we are all just running around amuck. What an oxymoron— an eating disorder facility without a nutritionist? That's like an Athletic Training Room without coaches tape, or an ophthalmologist office without glasses. My life is a joke. Maybe if I make it out of here, they'll make a movie adaptation of all of this mockery.

December 16
Day 11

So, today in Coping Skills, we had to make posters about the things that we are grateful for.

I wrote that I am grateful to my parents and family. I am grateful for their love, for their strength, and for their support. I hope that they think I'm strong, too. I hope they know I'm trying. It's time for another restaurant outing, and we're getting pasta. And you know what? I didn't think that it could get worse than Chinese. But alas. Here we are. Whenever I have anxiety over food, I try to break it down. Pasta is carbs, and so are apples, and so are carrots, and so are grapes. Just picture it as if you're eating apple noodles. Okay, I'm sorry. That sounds disgusting. But hey, whatever works, right?

I wonder if anyone else
feels as anxious
as I do.

I wonder if I'm alone.

December 17
Day 12

I got into a car accident on my way home last night.

Or maybe it was two nights ago. My days are becoming intertwined, and I just don't know anymore. To be honest, I don't even really remember what classes I went to this morning, but I think the accident was yesterday.

I don't know if I'll ever be able to admit to anyone what actually happened. I felt so faint when I was driving. My eyes were glassy and I couldn't stop thinking. But, I wasn't thinking about the road or the route. I was thinking about myself. I know that sounds ridiculous. I am so selfish and narcissistic. Images crashed through my mind, like passing waves at high tide. These images consisted of questions. What must it be like to be able to eat, and not hate yourself? What must it be like to not feel like such a failure all of the time? What must it be like to feel loved and valuable and deserving—even if just for a 32g serving of Skippy? Could there really be a world where I could look in the mirror, and not have my eyes well with tears over what I saw?

I thought about my day. Each one starts and ends like any other. I wake up at 5:30 am. Once I open my eyes, I pray. I ask God for the serenity to accept the things which I cannot change. I ask for the courage to change those things that I can. I ask for the wisdom to know the difference, and I ask that today be the day that I finally start living those words.

In high school, I had the same Spanish teacher for all 4 years: Señor Jorge Gomez. He started every single class with that prayer. He would tell us that the day that we stop learning will be the last day of our lives, even if it's not the day that we die. He also told us once that you should eat your vegetables first in any meal, because of nutrient absorption or something. He also believed that aliens abducted Steve Jobs in 2011. I think Gomez was a little crazy. I just like the prayer. That's all.

Anyway, after I pray, I get up. I walk across the room, and I take that long, hard stare in the mirror. I look at the reflection that magnified itself in my mind. When I look in the mirror, I don't see a person. I don't see a 5'5", curly-haired brunette. I don't see legs built to run, and to jump, and to explore all that life has to offer. I don't see arms made to heal and to create. I don't see a smile meant to be shared. When I look into the mirror, I see every horrible thought about myself plastered on my skin—like a thick, cemented shell. I see disgust and shame. I look at myself, and I understand why people run away at the sight of me. Who would want to be with someone who doesn't even want to be around herself? How could I blame them? Sometimes I wonder if maybe, just maybe, if I were to keep shrinking, one day I'd disappear. That way, no one will be able to see what I see.

But I guess I'm not here to give you my morning routine DIY tutorial. Back to yesterday. I tried to change lanes on the Merritt Parkway. I had class all morning, beginning at 8 am. And then, once my lab was dismissed at 2 pm, I had to begin my hour-long commute to treatment. Once treatment ended, I had to race home as quickly as possible to make it back to my dorm in time for my Res Life responsibilities. It's a lot. Sometimes I think it's too much. Sometimes I wish it would just stop. I'm exhausted.

And then, it happened. All I can remember was the sound of crackling glass and crippling plastic. I remember the feeling of fogginess and confusion when my head hit the steering wheel. It was late. Eight, maybe nine o'clock. But, it's funny. For some reason, I wasn't scared. I wasn't shocked. When I phased back into reality, I was alone. There was no noise shouting from the radio. No one was there to ask me if I was okay. Cars just drove around the shattered glass. The car I hit just pulled off to the side, activated its hazards, and parked. That was all. And for a brief moment, while absorbing it all, I couldn't help but wonder what would have happened if I had gotten hurt. What if something terribly awful had happened, and I was alone? Would anyone care? Would anyone pull over to see if I was okay? Would I, finally, for once, be able to take a sigh of relief? Could I finally be happy if it were all just over?

I've been thinking about that a lot lately: What if I didn't have to worry anymore? When I feel like that, I like to tell myself that "what if" are the worst two words in the English language. Sometimes that helps. Sometimes it doesn't.

December 18
Day 13

Dear God,

  I put my trust in You. I know how smart You are. You have molded me to be resilient and kind. I know that You are not plotting against me. I hope You know what You are doing here. You are trying your best to help me live the best life possible. I think I can say that surely... even though it's hard to believe sometimes. I'm sorry for not fueling Your creation. Please know what to do with all of this food that I'm eating. Please know how to manage these emotions that are flooding my being. Transform me into the beautiful image You imagined for me. I keep trying to remind myself that we are all made in Your image. That You did not place me on this Earth to shrink. I am strong. I am resilient. I am destined to flourish.

December 19
Day 14

A note to my future, struggling self:

  I know you are feeling horrible right now. Maybe
you just ate something that you think is "bad", or you
didn't do something "perfectly". Regardless of what it is
that sparked the emotion, I am so proud of you for
making it through... or for even just trying. You wouldn't
have been able to do that a few months ago, would you?
That's such incredible progress. Just know that, even
though this feeling is consuming you, it will pass. And, in
this very moment, you are kicking every ounce of self-
doubt to the curb. You are weakening it. The true,
happy, healthy, beautiful, loving, bright you is growing
stronger and more powerful.

  You may also be feeling guilty. You may be
feeling like a so-called "burden". It is so normal to feel
this way, but please remember that these are *feelings*.
They are not your innate being. These negative feelings
toward yourself do not define you. I can assure you that
no one is judging you. No one is thinking of you
differently. No one is angry with you. All they want to do
is love you, and support you. The people who love you...
the people that matter most... they want you to be happy.
They want you to be truly joyful. They do not want you
to exist in a world that is cursed by the pseudo-happiness
that your disordered thoughts make you believe in.

  <u>It may be difficult for you to believe, but you
deserve every ounce of care and compassion that this
world can offer.</u> You are not a burden. Read that

sentence again. And again. And again. Read that sentence until the words don't just look like ink blots on the page. Read it until you hear their meaning. You are a wonderful person. You are deserving of goodness and positivity. You are loved, and you deserve to feel that love. Allow love to pierce your steel-caged walls—the ones you built to brace yourself from heartache, disappointment, and damage. Allow the love to fill you until you are overflowing.

You may be feeling ashamed for any number of reasons. These feelings are 100% valid. But, I can assure you that you're a powerhouse of a human (you mitochondria, you). You have already conquered so much adversity, and you are strong enough to continue shining. You can do this. You are enough.

December 20
Day 15

INTUITIVE EATING

    *I*ntegration is important.

    *N*o reason to be ashamed.

    *T*ime is not an excuse to restrict yourself.

    *U*nderstand that change takes time.

    *I*t's normal to feel emotions.

    *T*ry your best.

    *I*n touch with your body. *I*dentify your triggers.

    *V*ulnerability. *V*ariety. *V*isualize happiness.

    *E*ngage actively.

    *E*agerly live.

    *A*llow yourself to participate in life.

    *T*rust your body.

    I am worthy.

    *N*ourish your spirit. *N*ourish your soul.

    *G*round yourself.

      This nutrition group is honestly such BS. The diet tech wanted us to come up with an acronym for intuitive eating. I just don't feel like intuitive eating is even a real concept. I think I'm just destined to live in this hell forever. Someone asked me the other day how I could be doing this to myself. How could I starve myself? How could I think straight? How could I possibly not even crave chocolate anymore?

      I thought back to past Easter mornings. Each year, I'd race down the stairs to see the chocolate bunnies and Reese's Peanut Butter Eggs that were awaiting me in my basket. When you start depriving yourself of something for so long, you forget. You forget about the happiness it used to bring you. You misplace the joy in those past memories. It's like when you lose a best friend. In the beginning, it sucks. You're miserable. All you can do is think about them, the times you shared, and the memories you made. You try to do something... anything... to distract yourself. Distraction is the only solace when you realize that reminiscing is almost as painful as the initial heartbreak itself.

Life doesn't stop, and soon, you will begin to think about them less and less often. Then, if you're lucky, those memories become less paralyzing and more nostalgic. You will get used to your new lifestyle without them.

When you become so engrossed in living out a certain, new lifestyle, you forget what it's like to be "normal" (or, what you used to consider "normal"). You forget your old habits. You fall into new customs. You adapt. I always thought that being "normal" was insulting, but wow I crave normalcy.

December 21
Day 16

December 22
Day 17

Today, I feel like a sheet of paper.

Blank. Flimsy. As though the wind could blow and I'd forever be lost. As though one wrong move, and I'll give someone a papercut. I am wrinkled. I'm trying, so desperately, to unfold myself. I'm impressionable to the slightest marking and scuff. I feel disposable.

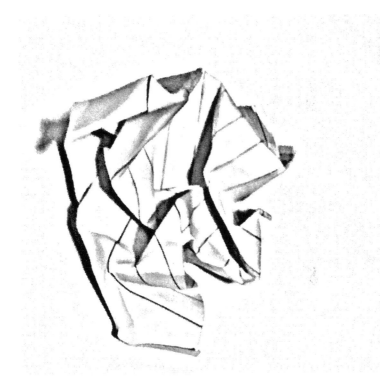

December 23
Day 18

Okay.

So, I've been going into the last three weeks of treatment with a really open mind. I think. But I'm tired of playing Ms. Nice Gal. I physically, emotionally, and conceptually cannot come to terms with why I am still here. I feel like I look exactly the same as I did at my highest weight. Sure, I dropped a few pants sizes, and a dress size or 3, but doesn't everyone from time to time? Those numbers are so subjective anyway. You can walk into one store and be a size 8 and walk into another and be a 00. With that being the reality that we live in, how am I supposed to believe anyone when they tell me that I am unhealthy?

My mom and best friend, Sara, keep on telling me that I don't see myself the way that others see me. That there is no *appearance* of an eating disorder. They say that it is futile to continue to orbit my universe around a particular appearance, or image. No matter what, my brain will not allow me to see myself as I am. Dr. Andrew said that the medication would help with the dysmorphia, but that was two medications, and three dosage increases ago.

I needed to prove them wrong. I needed to prove to them that maybe they were the ones who weren't seeing me properly. I went up to my room this morning to find an outfit to wear for Christmas Eve dinner. As I opened the center drawer of my dresser, I found the pants from my post-freshman 15. I read the label and swallowed a hard gulp of fear. I haven't tried these on in over a year. I dusted off the cobwebs of old memories in my mind. I tried to remember what it was like to go shopping with ease. What was it like to not care about needing to buy new jeans because your old ones were tight? I tried to remember the care-free thoughts of late-night pizza runs, the laughter, and bliss. I tried to remember what being happy used to feel like.

I pulled the jeans out of the drawer to find that they were as wrinkle-free and seamless as I remember my days used to be. Laying the fabric against my skin felt nostalgic. As if I was reaching out and holding onto a lost love. One leg at a time, I slipped the jeans on. I closed my eyes tightly, as if that would stop my reflection from staring back at me. As I buttoned the clasp, I fearfully opened one eye at a time. I was petrified that the image that would present before me would be as inadequate as I assumed.

When I looked in the mirror, I saw my legs swimming in a sea of denim. "Maybe they expanded in the wash?" I thought to myself. The material bagged itself over my kneecaps, like cascading waves. I shook my head in disgust. I have physical evidence that my vision is distorted. I have proof that I am not as I seem. Yet, the first thought that came to my mind was that of sheer disappointment. Why weren't these pants large enough so that they would fall off of my waist? Maybe I *am* lost at sea. Maybe this *isn't* healthy.

December 24
Day 19

The Ghost of Christmas Past.

I think I've always been a little bit insecure. I think I've always felt a little bit lonely. To me, success or wealth was solely based on quantity, and not on quality. It was about who had the highest test grades, the highest salary, the greatest number of friends. All of my life, it has been about numbers. It was about the number of dances I'd be performing in that year's recital, or about the number of clubs that I participated in at school. I stretched myself out so thin that I became perplexed as to why the number on the scale kept on growing. It was the single aspect of my life that didn't follow this "the greater the quantity, the greater the quality" relationship.

I hope that my siblings never fall into this trap. I hope that they never second guess their worthiness of love, respect, and success. I think I'm going to have to start reminding people that they are beautiful, and that they are loved, and that they are everything that is good in this world. People need to be validated… but that's a lot to ask from someone who cannot see those same qualities within herself.

I'm struggling. I feel dreary, and mellow, and blue. On days where the brightest thing I can see is the sun peeking through the piles of blankets I bundle myself under, I try to remember my childhood memories… especially the ones when my family would go to Disney World together. There, the sun penetrated the pores of my skin, and the biggest decision I had to make that day was which ride I wanted to venture to first. Now, the first decision I make each morning is whether or not I should just stay in bed and pray for tomorrow, or if I'll allow myself 28g of oatmeal instead of 26g.

December 25
Day 20

Merry Christmas.

I came across a post on Facebook saying:
"Like this if you're leaving 2017
thinner than when you entered it."
Cute.

Why is self-improvement, and assumption of happiness, sometimes measured in appearances? Why do we expect to obtain this essence of contentment when we achieve a certain "goal weight"? Where is the solace in fitting into the perfect pair of jeans? Or finally getting our dream promotion? Or getting accepted into our first-choice schools? Why does no one bother to ask: "Who is leaving this year with more self-love?", or "Who is leaving 2017 with a new friend? Or with a greater understanding of himself or herself?". We need to start asking: "Who is embarking on this new year with a realization of their purpose?"

Why do we settle for only the superficial? Why is everyone okay with this? How are we expected to fall in love with ourselves, and with the world, when our motivation derives from the opinions and perceptions of others?

At the end of the day, sure, you may achieve your dream weight, or get your dream job, or get into your graduate program. Sure, that happening may fill you with transient abundance. But, like a wave, that feeling will crash and pass. When the splendor wears off, you are left alone with yourself. You are the same version of yourself as before the event occurred. If you didn't like yourself before your achievement, odds are, your dissatisfaction will persist. We get caught up in this endless loop of trying to supplement our insecurities with materialistic and superficial "fillers". When we do this, we are only treating the symptoms. If we do not work towards helping the underlying, root cause of our self-resentment, any efforts are futile.

December 26
Day 21

My weight keeps rising, and I want to scream.
> I spent months torturing myself. I spent months in
> control. I was able to drop the weight with ease. Now,
> here I am. I am being forced to eat. I'm being forced to
> be fat again. Why is TFC doing this to me? How was it
> that I hated myself at my lowest weight? How did I think I
> was fat back then? What would my old-self say if she
> could see me now? I'm so disgusted with myself. I just
> want to be beautiful. I want to be able to love myself. I
> just can't even look in the mirror without crying. What
> are my friends going to say when I return to school? What
> are they going to think of me?

December 27
Day 22

Today was good.
It was better than yesterday.
It was a happy day.
I was determined to kick
This piece-of-garbage disorder
To the curb.
I followed my meal plan.
I was determined to find happiness.
I will no longer stand for this.
You know what? It's kind of funny.
I'm too weak to move,
>   but somehow I am able to grapple enough energy
>   to fit in some extra jumping jacks to burn off the
>   calories in my morning coffee.

I'm too weak to think,
>   yet I am able to spend hours daydreaming about
>   the meals I deprive myself of.

I'm too weak to feel,
>   yet I am still able to wallow in this insatiable pit
>   of indifference.

I've had enough.
I will not be weak.
I am not weak.

December 28

Day 23

I'm scared to go back to school. I'm scared
of *myself*. I'm a wildfire without the fiery
passion, and with double the destruction. I
need to find a support system. Here at home,
I have my family, but I don't want to burden
my friends. They didn't ask for this. They
didn't sign up to be my "sponsor". I can't
allow my distortions to continue to consume
my life. I need to make a conscious effort to
be there for my friends… and maybe they
will be there for me. I need to remember to
try my best to be happy. The psychiatrist has
increased my Zoloft dosage 3 times now.
And nothing. No change. No difference.
Maybe I'm not destined to be happy. Maybe
it's just not in the cards for me. Maybe I
should just start getting used to the fact that
I can't have it all.

isolation

December 29

Day 24

I'm having a low right now.

I don't know what happened. At dinner, I was fine. Dad
and I were getting along. He even said, "I love when
you're like this". Wow. Maybe that meant that I was
becoming my old self again—the happy, energetic
Kirsten that I miss so much.

But, oh well. That daydream was interrupted the second I
got hungry. Immediately, I hated myself again. The
physical manifestation of my internal hollowness is
petrifying. I can't stand the feeling of existing in this void
shell.

December 30
Day 25

In 2018, I can improve my life by being kinder to my soul. That is such a lame answer, but it's true. I wish that I could focus on the things that truly matter. Instead, my mind is over-consumed with the daunting reminders of weight, shape, and size. I wish I could be able to give myself the love, kindness, and compassion that people keep telling me that I deserve. Life is the worst. I'm so angry. I can't believe how this year turned out. I hope that I'll wake up from this miserable nightmare sometime soon. I feel as though I'm in a hopeless rut.

They upped my meal plan again today. Are we kidding?! They just want me to get fat. I mean, I'm already halfway back to my pre-sick weight. I feel like such a failure. I feel like I'm always compliant at meals, so why is it that my plan needs to be bumped up? It's not fair.

Maybe in the new year, I can have some ounce of self-respect and self-control. Why am I so sad all of the time? Remember freshman year, when you couldn't fall asleep without a smile on your face? Now here you are, driving sixty miles, each and every day, for treatment. Your only responsibilities are to do well in school and to be happy. C'mon! That's so easy! Why can't you just do that?! That's so embarrassing.

Okay okay okay. How am I supposed to uphold this New Years Resolution if that is how I speak to myself? If that's how I treat myself, how am I supposed to expect others to treat me differently? Do I want them speaking to me with profanity and distaste? Or with love and compassion?

Please choose yourself in this new year. Fall in love with yourself in this new year. Find peace with your past in this new year. Be kind... not only to others, but to yourself. Just as the wellbeing of those around you holds the highest importance, yours counts, too.

You matter, okay?

December 31
Day 26

I remember last New Years Eve.

I wasn't in my disordered mindset yet. I was able to enjoy the desserts and the company, and I was happy. I will not allow myself to continue derailing.

(More) New Years Resolutions:

1. ~~Stop hating myself~~ Love myself
2. ~~Stop restricting myself~~ Nourish myself
3. Get discharged
4. Find something new, that makes me happy
5. Remember to list my gratitudes, daily
6. ~~Be happy~~ Try your best to be happy
7. Study more
8. Try to be a better friend
9. Start singing again
10. Keep writing when you're sad
11. Be more assertive
12. Smile more
13. Stop using the word "hate"
14. Discontinue negative self talk
15. Read positive quotes daily
16. Be the sunshine you need

JANUARY

THE STORM

January 1
Day 27

Your track Record for making it through days like today is 100%, and I think those odds are very good. Keep on fighting, warrior ♡

January 2
Day 28

You are exactly where you are supposed to be.

January 3
Day 29

Conceptual Happiness.

So, we're all just living a journey, right? It's the paradigm of the human experience. Human beings tell the story of their lives through everyday interactions and experiences. Part of me is trying to figure out what kind of story I'm writing.

I don't know if I believe that I could be a happy story. I mean, sure, my mood has been gradually getting better. I don't know. Maybe this whole "happiness" thing is a bit overrated. Ultimately, I think that's what everyone wants—happiness… but people spend their whole lives searching for this virtue like a straw of hay in a world filled with needles. Through each puncture, and each wound, we keep gravitating towards the dream that, if they were to just try again, maybe they won't get bruised.

I think I read somewhere that Aristotle believed that the virtue of flourishing should be practiced. It should be experienced, and it should be exercised. But can it even really be taught? Can you learn how to be happy?

When I think of learning something, I think of outlines, and lists of things to evaluate to ensure that you're staying on track. How am I supposed to learn something without parameters, or guidelines? How will I know if I'm on the right track? How will I know if I'm improving?

January 4
Day 30

I wish I could see myself as beautiful.
I wish I could see myself
as more than my mind
allows me to see.
I had a life imagined for myself
that was so much greater than this
hell
that I am merely surviving.

January 6
Day 32

Being Recovered.

If someone were to wave a wand, making me magically recovered, I would know. I would know because my mind wouldn't be grossly over-consumed with thoughts of weighing "x" amount, or with plans of my perfect "cheat" day. My life without an eating disorder would be extravagant. I would wake up to the sound of birds chirping, and not to the sound of my stomach growling. I would rise from my bed and run to hug my sister good morning. Instead, I run to the scale, whose value will determine whether my next few hours will involve having breakfast or not.

I'd be able to go on walks without concern that my legs may give out from under me. I'd be able to go out with my friends and family with ease. No longer will I have to turn down a post-chapter coffee run, or 2 am pizza-delivery study breaks, or my boss' famous snickerdoodle pie. I will be allowed to smile for joy, as opposed to hoping that utilizing my facial musculature will burn off an extra calorie or two. I can allow myself abundant happiness.

January 7
Day 33

1/7/18

I want you to know how grateful I am to have met you on this journey & to have received your support, love, & empathy. ♥ You are such an intelligent, wise, caring, beautiful young woman & I am so thankful to know you.

I know this battle isn't easy, but you are a powerful warrior - never forget how much courage & strength you have inside of you. I have so much faith that you will overcome your obstacles & win this fight. ♥ I am so so proud of you & for continuing to push through even when things get really tough. You've got this, girl! I love you so so much.

January 8
Day 34

Gratitudes

I am thankful that I have a family that cares. Although they don't understand, they try to. We had Tio Luis' surprise retirement party today. He told me that he has been praying for me each morning. That he hopes that, each day, I wake up. He hopes that, even if I am not feeling like it, that I push through. It was interesting that he told me this. He and I never really had a deep conversation before. And to be honest, it made me feel so vulnerable. Am I really that sick that someone, whom I barely ever speak to, feels worrisome for me?

January 9
Day 35

The Fire.

I built you a fire
When I was in the seventh grade.
And I filled it high
With all sorts of flammable things.
You know,
Like woods chips,
And lint balls,
And Doritos.

And once I ran out
Of those minuscule fire-starters,
I went on a search.
I searched for something,
Anything,
To feed this monster
That we cannot seem
To live without.

Something that would fuel you...
Some sort of mass ammunition.
And I prayed that you wouldn't turn to smoke.
Because, you know.
Why would it be the fire's fault
For burning out?
You were the one
Who was supposed to feed it.
And you thought

The fire was there
To give you warmth?
To serve you as
A guiding light?

Oh, sweetheart.
Fire doesn't work that way.
Life doesn't work that way.

And so you go on your mission.
You search for something,
Anything,
That will feed this demon enough
To last the night.

Because
To you,
It's better to be burned
Than to be left in the dark.

You see,
If you burn,
It means you were touched.
If you were touched,
It means you were taking up space.
If you were taking up space,
Maybe,
Just maybe,
That means that the world still has some room for you.

So you begin to think.

You think of the things
That once started a fire in *you*.
You know,
Like afternoon baseball games,
And weekend BBQs,
And a room to run to when
You found the dark
Chasing after you.

And these thoughts turned to dreams
Somewhere when you traded
Your matchbox for a lighter.
But, now,
How am I supposed to light a fire with a syringe?

So you use your dreams.
And like a tank of gasoline,
You pour them onto this nearly burnt-out flame.
You give it all you have left.
Every last drop,
Until you are empty.

You see,
In feeding the flame,
To keep your fear alive,
You ran yourself dry.

You were too afraid
To stop yourself from shrinking,
Because you were afraid
To run into the dark.

But, honey,
The darkness found its way
Inside of you.

January 10
Day 36

I feel this overwhelming sense of emptiness.
     As though I am suffocating.
     As if every breath I wish to take,
     takes the effort of the unimaginable.
     I feel undercooked.

January 11
Day 37

Life can be so invalidating sometimes.

I'm trying to figure out why all of this started. Why did I feel the need to lose weight? Why did I find analgesia in portion control and restriction?

I was pretty fit my whole life. In high school, I ate whatever I wanted, and generally maintained the same weight. I didn't necessarily like the number on the scale, but was it debilitating? No. Is *anyone* satisfied with their weight at that age? Probably not, considering the culture we live in today. Would seeing the number on the scale each morning paralyze me? No.

I danced for hours on end each night. I appreciated my body for its strength and power. I never thought twice about the calories in my favorite pasta dish, or about the grams of Cheerios, I poured into my breakfast bowl.

I don't think I know a single person who is 100% happy with their appearance, and I think that's okay. Natural, even. If we were all totally content with ourselves, we would not have the motivation to achieve higher. Or to reinvent ourselves. Or to further ourselves along this journey.

When I began losing weight back in June, I reached out to my pediatrician. I mean, dropping weight so quickly? Concerning, right? It was a cry for help. She validated the concerns of my speedy weight loss by weighing me. I knew that my actions and behaviors were unhealthy. I just needed someone. I needed someone to tell me that this wasn't normal. I needed someone to tell me that I shouldn't be weighing myself all of the time, or that I shouldn't be constantly daydreaming over my next meal. How should I know that it's obsessive to weigh out each drop of food to the closest gram? Doesn't everyone hate themselves?

To my doctor, I was doing "great". She was so proud of me for finally "getting healthy". She thought I'd found the *secret*. Was it cutting out carbs? Was it switching to smaller portion sizes? I laughed as the voice inside of my head whispered:

> "Try a cocktail of crippling depression,
> self-loathing, and dysmorphia".

And it wasn't until I needed to get an updated TB test in August that she'd see me again. As I walked into her office, 30 lbs lighter than my previous visit, her eyes filled with fear. Before even asking me why I was there, she told me to step on the scale. In disbelief, her voice shook as she read the number out loud. She told me I was going to die. She told me that I wasn't allowed to go back to school. She ordered bloodwork, to be done immediately. She asked me "Why would you do this to yourself?"

I thought that was funny. You know, as if this was the future I decided for myself. As if this was a reality that I hand-picked. As if this was a choice.

In spite of her wishes, I went back to school. The disordered voice, that rang through my ears, became louder and louder. I still couldn't see it. I still can't. In my eyes, when I look in the mirror, I still see the washed-up high school girl who gained the "freshman 15". And, with all of the feedback I was getting, how could I stop? I got so many compliments. My friends asked me if I lost weight. They asked me how I did it. That must have meant that they thought I looked good, right? How was I supposed to know that those words were derived from a place of concern? So, I kept going. I kept restricting. I substituted meals for naps. Snacks for extra study sessions in the library. I picked up extra clinical hours and research opportunities. I did anything to distract myself from the mental and physical pain I was inflicting on myself.

I remember back in September when my mom held a mini-intervention. I started going home less and less, out of fear that my parents would say something about the weight I continued to lose. My mom eventually told me that, if I didn't find a counselor to talk to, she was going to pull me out of school.

So, I found a counselor. When I contacted the secretary to make an appointment, I told the woman that I felt as though I may have an eating disorder. I told her that I had dropped a little bit of weight over the last few months. I told her about the fact that I was sad all of the time, and that I hadn't been able to get through a day without crying. I told her about the anxiety that crawled through each crevice of my skin. I told her that I just needed someone to talk to. The woman gave me an appointment with a counselor (let's call this counselor: Mrs. Short). Shorty had been working with disordered eating clients for years and years. The secretary told me that I was in good hands.

You see, the thing is that I don't ask for help. I don't. It's just not my thing. Ms. Independent by Kelly Clarkson had been my anthem since I discovered that I could use a hairbrush as a microphone to serenade my stuffed animals. And, after the appointment was over, I had no reason to ever want to ask for help from anyone again.

I got to the appointment around 40 minutes early. I pulled into the parking lot and found a spot in the back. In the 80° weather, I still had my car's heater blasting. I contemplated just driving back to my apartment. "I don't have a problem," my disordered voice reverbed in my mind, "why are you wasting this woman's time?" I shook off the voice, took a deep breath, applied a new coat of my red lipstick, and got out of my car before I had a chance to think twice about it.

I anxiously sat in the waiting room. I was still wearing my clinical clothes. I prayed that none of my clients would see me here. "Strong people don't need help", the voice of my demons sang in tune. Short-Stuff called me into her office before the voices could come up with more libel. The room mimicked that of my mom's home office. There was a mahogany desk, and she sat in one of those office chairs that you dream about owning as a kid. You know what I'm talking about—the one you can spin around and around and around in. On her walls hung photos of Shorty with her husband and her children. She had framed her many accolades and diplomas. Heaps of papers were stacked on the desk in disarray. It reminded me of an accumulation of snowfall on a ski resort's hill. I always thought it was funny. Snow is comprised of a single, minuscule snowflake. Yet, when they join forces, they become dense, supportive, and sturdy. I took a sigh of relief. Maybe, just maybe, I am in good hands. Maybe she could be the supportive union I need right now. Maybe I'm meant for more than this lonesome life.

Short-Cake asked me to take a seat in the Lazy-Boy that was situated diagonally from her desk. She took a deep breath and asked me why I had come in today. I glared at her. Why *was* I here? Well, a statue can only take so much weight before it collapses. What if I am the final snowflake, which causes the avalanche. What if I am the last piece of the puzzle—the piece that causes everything to collapse. I immediately began to cry. These weren't any of those cute Hallmark tears. This was ugly sobbing. It was the type of sobbing which makes it impossible to catch your breath.

"If I saw my sister doing this to herself,"
I mumbled under my breath,
"I don't think I could live with myself."
The councilor took a long look at me. She handed me a box of tissues, and eagerly scanned my file. She questioned me about the specifics of my weight loss. She asked me about my behaviors, my eating patterns, my body image, and lastly, my weight.

"Sweetheart," she said in a polite, but almost condescending, tone, "I have been working with patients with disordered eating for nearly fifteen years now. I have to be honest with you. You just don't look to me like you have an eating disorder."

I laughed. "See?" the disordered voice said, as it laughed in my ears, "Even she knows you're too fat to be sick!" I froze as I sank deeper and deeper into the folds of the recliner. I laughed in disbelief at what was happening.

67

Can she say that? Can she invalidate someone like that? Maybe she's right? I mean, maybe I *am* too fat. Maybe she sees myself as I see my reflection. Maybe the mirror isn't lying to me. Maybe everyone is telling me that I lost weight to make me feel better about the fact that I've actually gained weight. Maybe Shorty's right. Maybe I'm crazy.

Who needs an avalanche, anyway. She smiled back at me with a toothy grin. "Huh," she breathed, "You know what? Something that I've noticed, in a few of my anorexic patients, is that their teeth look too big for their face". I stood there, perplexed. "And you know what?" she continued, "I see it now. Yours look a little too big on you, too".

And just like that, the very last part of me shattered. With that comment went all essences of self-confidence I had left. I stood up slowly. "Maybe I'm dreaming." I thought, "Maybe if I stand up, I'll fall and wake up from this nightmare, back in my bed". But, as my feet made contact with the cherry stained linoleum floors, I knew that this truly was happening. I collected my backpack, and without losing eye contact with the door, I walked out of her office. As I walked past the secretary, I heard her speak "Honey, do you want to schedule a follow-up?" Unphased, I continued walking. Slowly, I left the building. I walked through the parking lot. I walked to my car. I sat in the driver's seat, gracefully, as if I was trying not to make a single sound. I grabbed hold of the steering wheel. I closed my eyes and took a deep breath—hoping that I could inhale reminders of goodness, and exhale the hatred that loomed inside of me. But, when I opened my eyes, I was the same. Nothing had changed. I was still a snowflake trying to keep cold on that warm September day. I carefully rested my forehead on the steering wheel, between my hands, and cried.

January 12
Day 38

Who is your most authentic self?

A day as my most authentic self would involve waking up as late as I'd like, as opposed to opening my sleep-filled eyes to the first crack of daylight, in hopes of fitting in as many steps as possible. I could go out with my friends without the petrifying fear of what they would say if my stomach rolled through my shirt. I could go out with my friends without the anxiety of how I should restrict my calories throughout the day, in case one of the girls decides to end the night with ice cream or hot chocolate. I could laugh again. I could *really* laugh - not just that fake laughter I've been echoing for so long. I could experience that laughter that leaves you breathless—and maybe that would feel as breathless as the relief of accepting my imperfections would be.

January 13
Day 39

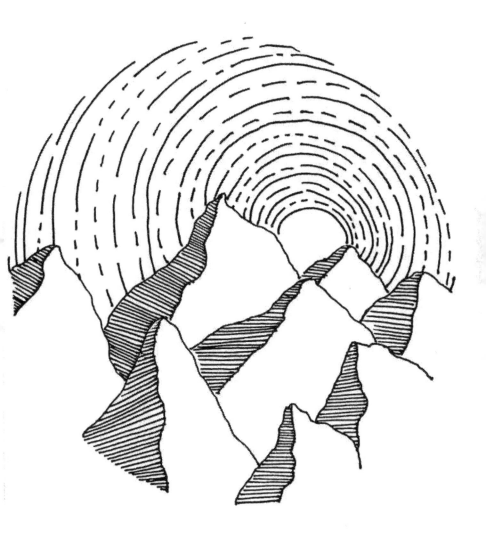

January 14
Day 40

Sometimes, leaving can feel good.

Pure, even.

That is if you're abandoning something that was once important to you.

Something that once mattered to you.

Leaving allows you to pull out pieces of your life by the stem.

Like a weed in the garden.

But you cannot do that until your life has planted roots.

January 15
Day 41

There are points where I find myself stopping in time.
I become aware of all of these simple
surroundings and begin to pray. I pray in hopes that these
exact moments will remain in my memory forever. I sit
here, yearning to recall the most minuscule moments of
my life. For, aren't these the moments that will shape us
into the people we are destined to become?

They say that with every recollection, a memory
will change ever-so-slightly in your mind. I think this is
the sheer reason why some find it difficult to extract the
origins of their deepest, most innate fears.

Your body clings to these life-altering
experiences, whilst they're in their purest, most natural
form. In doing so, your mind causes these moments to be
wiped from your memory, and instead, imprinted on
your soul.

January 16
Day 42

I'm freaking out.

I can't breathe.

It's like the walls are closing in.

I just woke up from a nightmare.

I looked like Violet from Willy Wonka and the Chocolate Factory.

I can't eat breakfast.

I can't eat lunch.

I can't eat.

I can't do this.

I feel suffocated by the voices in my head.

I just want to go back to sleep.

I'm going back to sleep.

God, please let me wake up from this living nightmare.

January 17
Day 43

I had a bad day yesterday.

It was my first day of the spring semester, and to Dianne's astounding discretion, my first day off from treatment. I was so motivated. So ready to get back into the swing of my life.

But, when I woke up, every ounce of motivation was eliminated. I didn't allow myself to eat breakfast. Then, I didn't allow myself to eat lunch. Instead, I took joy in dwelling in the sounds of my grumbling stomach. It was like music to my ears, and God, that makes me sound absolutely sick.

I decided to follow my meal plan for dinner. After, I was so overcome by the loudness of my self-deprecating thoughts that I took melatonin and fell fast asleep by 8:00 pm. Sleep is my only grace from the thoughts that invade and echo through my shell of a body.

I went to bed with all of the intentions of waking up tomorrow morning and hitting the "restart" button. I was going to be compliant, and I was going to eat. But when I woke up, the voices were screaming louder than I had ever heard before. The only way to escape them is by listening to them. Believing that I'm fat. That I don't need the extra calories that breakfast, or lunch, entails. Now, I'm sitting here in TFC and Jane is playing "Hey There Delilah" on her ukelele and I don't know if I can do this. This is not the life I imagined for myself. Why am I here? God, why are You allowing my mind to abuse me like this? Where are You, now that I need You the most? I don't know if I can keep this going. I feel like I'm falling apart. The walls are closing in on me, and I can't breathe. I just want this to be over.

How am I supposed to make it through the semester like this?

January 21
Day 47

Why. Why. Why.

       I just don't understand why my body hates me. I'm convinced the TFC is keeping me here because they just want to watch me get fat.

       Maybe I'll put all of these journal entries together and title it: *I hate myself: a memoir.*

January 22

Day 48

<u>D B T skills</u>   Jan 22, 2018

A ·· activities ·· in-the-moment distractions to take
              your mind off your negativity

C ·· contributing ·· what can you do in the moment
              to contribute to something
              outside of yourself, to remove
              yourself from your inner negativity

C ·· comparison ·· compare the things you do
              have, and what you are grateful
              for.

E ·· emotions ·· acting opposite to your current
              emotional state

T ·· thoughts ·· fact check / proofs

P ·· pushing away ·· push away that thought
              and visualize the opposite

S ·· sensations ·· smell flowers, use frozen orange,
              drink tea or coffee or water,
              run hands under cold / hot
              H_2O

Ride The Wave; it crashes and passes

82

January 23
Day 49

Life has been hard.

I got into a fight with mom. I lied and told her that I had clinical today, even though I didn't. I just wanted to be alone. I just feel so guilty. She has other things to worry about, other than me. I'm 20 years old. An adult. She shouldn't have to deal with this. I'm not a child anymore. She didn't ask for this. No one did. Why can't I just be normal? I feel like a failure. I feel like a failure as a daughter. I feel like a failure as a friend. Even my therapist told me that I probably put on a "stand-off*ish*" attitude. No wonder no one cares about me. I hate this illness. Each day is a battle. I don't want to get out of bed anymore. I don't want to shower. I don't want to go to class. I don't want to eat.

The voice in my head is just so loud and I need it to shut the hell up.

I don't know how much longer I can live day-to-day like this.

January 24
Day 50

I feel like a pig.

It is taking everything in me not to just drive back home to Long Island right now. I can't do this. Everyone is looking at the weight I've gained so far in treatment. They're all judging me. They're probably talking about how fat I've gotten. I wish someone would just hug me and tell me that it's going to be okay. I can't do this right now. My suitemate made cookies and dropped one off in my room. I wanted to put it back on the tray in the kitchen, but I felt like she would have noticed. What if she got mad at me? I can't lose any more people in my life right now. I already feel so ostracized. I feel like everyone knows my darkest secrets. I feel like everyone was so compassionate when I initially shared about my illness, but now I feel like a painting in an art museum.

Everyone just looks at me, and then walks along. When was the last time you went to the MoMA and stopped to ask what thoughts raced through the artists head while developing their "work of art". What if Van Gogh painted Starry Night as a distraction from his inner demons? And, all this time, we just stare in splendor, when in reality, the painting was just a cry for help?

January 25
Day 51

I am just really, really sad today.

I feel like I am in a fishbowl.

Every noise around me sounds washed out and faint.

My eyes feel like they are covered in plastic film.

I feel numb.

I sat myself down in my room this afternoon.

I wanted to drive home, but I didn't have the energy.

At 3:45 pm, I wanted to go to sleep for the rest of the night.

I just want to feel *anything* other than this pain.

January 26
Day 52

Note To Self:

So, I know.

I know you're struggling right now. I know that this is hard and miserable and unfair. I know there are some moments that seem hopeless. Like, why should you even try? Well, here are 10 reasons why:

1. To be happy again.
    a. Think to a point in the depths of your disorder. A point when nothing could tear you apart from your bed. Not even your books could bring you joy anymore. Since you've begun recovery, you've smiled again. And, oh, how long it's been.

2. To be careless again.
    a. Think to when your roommate asked you if you would like a bite of her homemade bagels. How you didn't have to hesitate to try it. How the first thought that came to your mind was how delicate and fluffy it was—and not how many calories the bite consisted of.

3. To make memories again.
    a. Think about when Jackson came to visit. How he wanted to share some nachos over some reminiscent conversation at

the diner. Remember how much fun you had? How much joy that evening brought you? Remember how a few chips didn't cause you to blow up like a balloon? Remember, you can trust your body. Your body knows what to do with the energy you provide it with.

4. To be at peace.
    a. Recall the moment at mass when Father Rich and mom and dad and your brother and sister prayed over you. Think about your conversation with God. He is carrying you on this battlefield.

5. For the moments that take your breath away.
6. For future happiness.
    a. I promise it will follow.

7. For your future children.
8. For your parents.
9. For your siblings.
10. For yourself.
    a. Now is your time to shine. It is time for you to be your own role model. It is your time to flourish. Allow yourself to flourish.

At the end of time, remember that you'll approach the gates of Heaven with nothing but the clothes on your back. You will never be judged by the size of your waist or your arms or your thighs. You will be judged by the kindness in your heart. You will be judged by the happiness you have cultivated. You will be judged by the lives you have touched.

God created you in His own image, and that image is absolutely gorgeous.

January 27
Day 53

Birthday Festivities.

Charlotte had a celebratory birthday dinner last night. I looked at the menu beforehand. My mind began to race. What would the lowest-calorie option be? Why couldn't she have chosen a restaurant with the nutritional facts on the menu? What is the safest choice I can make? I sat next to Lynn at the table, which was decked with girls whose eyes glimmered with hope, and whose smiles were so authentic. I marveled at her authenticity. How is it possible for someone to be so genuinely happy? How can I find that?

I asked Lynn how her roommates were doing; if they were getting along; if things were running smoothly. Lynn seemed relieved with how the semester was playing out, but hesitated for a moment.

She began to tell me of a story where she and the bunch went out to dinner. Lynn scanned the menu, and honed in on a delicious looking salad. When asked by one of the roommates what she was preparing to order, Lynn read off the menu's description of the meal. She then received a disgusted look from the crew.

"We don't order salads", they all said in unison. Lynn took a step back. If she wanted a salad, then she'd get a salad. If she wanted a cheeseburger, she'd order a cheeseburger. She couldn't understand why she was being judged for honoring her body's cravings. She couldn't understand why she was being judged for trusting her body. She didn't bother with their discouragement, and despite the eye rolls and snarky comments, she ordered the salad. She understood that these people are not embedded in her psyche. She is her own person, and that is perfectly okay. She explained that she has so many friends, family, and love in her life. Just because her roommates don't particularly treat her with the utmost compassion doesn't mean much. It doesn't change her zest for life. She will continue to do what makes her happiest, regardless of the opinions of others.

I aspire to be like her someday. I aspire to be unapologetically myself. To be unshaken by judgments. To live a life of growing joy, as opposed to a life with aspirations to shrink.

I'm really afraid that my sister may look at my habits and follow in my footsteps. I think that she is the most beautiful girl in the world, and I am so scared that she will grow up, and not be able to see that in herself. That is such a great motive for recovery—to serve as a role model. To be strong enough to redirect disordered comments. To remind her that: life is about flourishing, and not about withering.

Do it for her. Do it for Lynn. Do it for identity. Do it to inspire. Do it to change their lives and yours. Keep fighting each and every day. Strive to be happier in all of life's moments. Choose joy.

January 29
Day 55

I had Chapter last night.

Afterwards, I walked out of the building with our advisor. She asked me how I was feeling. I feel like that was a little bit of a joke. How am I feeling? Well, where do I begin...

How about the horrid self-loathing?

Or how I can't even think about my weight without crying?

How I had to cover my mirror with a towel, because I can't stand to look at myself?

How about the distress of trying to balance school, and treatment, and friends, and greek life, and student government, and work?

How about balancing all of those whilst not being able to focus on anything entirely?

I mean, try reading a page of your favorite novel, while your partner is screaming abusive slander into your ear. I digress. Asking an anorexic how they are feeling is not the best choice of words.

January 30
Day 56

My Life in Six Chapters:

 Chapter 1:

 I'm six years old, standing on a dining
room chair in the kitchen. My eyes are just level
with the KitchenAid mixer, as my mom hands me
the spoon. I curl up on the sofa and take a
wholesome gulp of the batter as I watch the
Thanksgiving Day Parade. Mmm. Chocolate
pudding. My favorite.

 Chapter 2:

 I'm twelve years old, pacing around the
kitchen as my mother cracks eggs into the mixer.
I ponder over which foods I will try first at
Thanksgiving dinner. Will it be the mashed
potatoes in a well of gravy? Or maybe the
cranberry sauce from the tin can? My mother
hands me the mixing spoon, and I ask her if she'd
like to share.

 "No thank you," she said, "I'm not eating
until dinner".

I watch the parade and I wonder if the Rockettes
are skipping their favorite treats, too.

 Chapter 3:

 I'm seventeen years old, and I go into
Manhattan on Thanksgiving morning, while my
mom bakes at home. I notice that the balloons are
a lot smaller, and less vibrant in person. The
celebrities are, too.

Chapter 4:

I'm twenty years old, and my mom doesn't cook on Thanksgiving anymore. I spent dessert sipping on diet soda while my brother scooped into the chocolate pudding. "Mmm," he says. It's his favorite now.

Chapter 5:

I'm twenty-five years old, and Thanksgiving is at my home this year. My mom brought her famous pudding cake. There is a lighthearted spirit in the conversation, and I decide to take a bite. "Mmm," I thought "that wasn't as scary as I remember".

Chapter 6:

She's six years old, standing on a dining room chair in the kitchen. Her eyes are just level with the KitchenAid mixer, as I hand her the spoon. She cuddles up on the sofa and takes a wholesome gulp of the batter as she watches the Thanksgiving Day Parade. I curl up next to her with a spoon of my own. She's my favorite now.

January 31
Day 57

Maybe this time,
the rain can fall
instead of you.

FEBRUARY

THE ROOTING

February 1
Day 58

I once heard someone say,
    "You should be unapologetically yourself".
    I guess that makes sense.
    If we were all meant to be exactly the same,
    Wouldn't we be?
    Wouldn't we all have the same sized jeans?
    Wouldn't we all have the same favorite color?
    Wouldn't life just be incredibly boring?

    But,
    What if I don't want to stick out?
    What if I don't like myself?
    What if I wanted to just disappear?

"The meek
shall do
some
Earth-inhereting"

SHOWER ME with YOUR MERCY

bloom where you are planted

February 4
Day 61

Two Months.

Today marks two months since my first day of treatment. Since then, I've had a lot of time to find my voice. I have encountered many people who look down on those who struggle every day. Those who condescend the individuals who fight for the will-power to make it through another hour, minute, or second in recovery.

To those people, I swear to you... I'm trying.

When I look in the mirror, I *try* to see what I love about myself. I *try* to see the good. But, my inner light is buried under heaps of blanketed malice. The imperfections I see are crippling. They initiate panic and overconsuming fear. My reflection captures a visual manifestation of my eating disorder. While the number on the scale keeps dropping, I still see the same body I've always lived in. It's like looking in a FunHouse mirror. Except, instead of your body being stretched and contorted in a comical manner, the image relayed back to me is one that I recognize. One that doesn't seem so foreign to me. One that I believe in.

I still have so much of this battle left to fight, but I am getting closer and closer each day. I promise that I'm trying.

February 5
Day 62

The Game.

It's literally as if it came out of a movie. There was a basketball game at school today. My friends wanted me to go. It was at 9 pm, so I knew that I would be able to get there right after treatment. I really didn't want to go. I just wanted to go home and sleep. I don't care that it's only 9 o'clock. I don't care that I have an essay due tomorrow, or a test next week. Sleep means that I don't have to stay awake with these thoughts of self-loathing and sadness.

I texted my friends back and forth. I came up with every excuse in the book as to why I wouldn't be able to make it. They didn't want to hear it. They begged me to come... to at least stay until halftime. So, I did. I donned my favorite Women's Basketball hoodie and walked to the gym.

I was there before my friends had arrived. I reserved a row at the top of the bleachers. I made my way up the wooden steps, hoping that my footsteps didn't make too much noise. I prayed that those around me didn't gag at how fat I looked today. It's funny. As more and more people began filling up the gymnasium, I felt more and more alone. I felt this overwhelming sense of paranoia... as if everyone around me could see the inner, self-deprecating dialogue that rang through my ears:

"Even in this hoodie, you look fat."

"Here you are, watching your favorite sport with your favorite people, and you're still not happy."

101

"You're such a bore."

"No wonder you feel this way."

"Maybe if you didn't eat lunch today, you
wouldn't have had the energy to go out tonight,
and maybe you wouldn't be so miserable."

"Maybe if you hadn't eaten dinner, you'd be
pretty enough to be having a good time."

The internal, one-sided conversation was
interrupted as the home team shot a 3-pointer. Everyone
in the bleachers was on their feet—screaming, chanting,
clashing their noise-makers. The marching band's
trumpets roared, and the players' sneakers scuffed and
squeaked as they danced for joy on the court. Bells were
ringing, fans were whistling, my friends were stomping
their feet.

And still, I felt numb. It was as if I wasn't even
there. As if I wasn't present in my body. It was as if I was
watching myself from the stands, mocking at the misery
that paralyzed me.

I couldn't take it.

I left without saying goodbye.

I walked back to my apartment.

In the freezing February night, I refused to wear
my jacket.

Anything would feel better than this.

I hoped that the bitter cold would numb me.

I hoped that it would freeze me from this flaming
nightmare.

February 6
Day 63

If you use your eating disorder for control & power, Could you imagine how power-ful you'd feel if you contro-lled your eating disorder ?

February 7

Day 64

I am in a very dark place — February 7, 2018
right now. I need to wake up from this
nightmare. I have no motivation. No compassion.
No desire for love or affection or friendship or
successes or emotion. I don't even feel the dull
hunk of numbness anymore. I simply just "don't"

February 9
Day 66

I'm Angry.

  I'm so pissed off with my treatment team. Diane is fake, and a liar, and a witch with a capital 'B'. I'm so over her telling me that I'm "fine". I *know* I'm not "fine". I'm crying out for help. Begging. Making myself so vulnerable. She doesn't listen. Nobody listens. I'm screaming for help in a deaf world.

  I just want someone to hold me and tell me that this is all going to be okay. I want my mom and my dad. I want my grandma. I just don't want to be here. I feel like an absolute failure. Sure, I have restored my weight, but I feel as though I am in a worse mental state than I've ever been in before. All these emotions that I've used restriction to numb are finally resurfacing. They are suffocating me.

  No one tells you about this part. No one talks about the emotions after weight-restoring. How, when you start refeeding and healing your brain, all of the suppressed emotions reemerge tenfold. How, when your body is physically healed, your mental state hasn't even begun the restoration process.

  I hate this. I hate being sad. I hate the screaming thoughts. I hate hating myself and my body. I just want to breathe. I need to get out of here. I need this to stop. I need to get better so that I can get away from my therapist and other toxic, toxic souls.

  Today, I finally got a chance to talk to a dietician. It's about time. I haven't seen a dietician in two weeks, which sounds like an actual joke considering that this is a treatment facility for people who need considerable, regular nutritional counseling. She was kind. She validated the fact that I have restored my weight and that I am in maintenance. Which is okay, whilst completely not okay at the same time.

On one hand, the numbers on the scale make me nauseous. I wasted 6 months of my life compressing myself. I yearned to become so small, that maybe one day I'd disappear. Now, here I am. I am back in stability, as if none of that had ever happened. I mean, I guess it's a relief that I'm in maintenance. I have been feeling as though I have been blowing up like a balloon... like a monster. Knowing that I have achieved a setpoint, whilst allowing myself to eat foods which I enjoy, makes me happy.

I keep trying to remember my 20th birthday. That day was the last time I can remember being truly happy. I got to spend the day with all of my loved ones. My sibling's dance recital was that afternoon. I felt so needed. I was able to help my sister, and her friends, get their makeup done, and their costumes situated. How important I felt when all of my old teammates and dance instructors embraced me with hugs and "Happy Birthday" wishes. How loved I felt. I want to be back there so badly. I miss the old, motivated, happy me. I hope she is still there. Hopefully, she's just buried underneath this disorder. I'm over it. I think today is the push that I needed.

February 10
Day 67

"Hope"?

Today, I asked in group:

"How do I improve my body image?"

Another client responded:

"Don't bother, it only gets worse from here".

HAHAHA.

AWESOME.

February 11
Day 68

The Journey

> And while each day presents
> With a brand new light,
> Reminders of yesterday
> Will continue to loom.
> Yesterday's moon
> Will shed a light of its own,
> To remind us of the pain,
> Darkness,
> Silence,
> That will inevitably come.
>
> It's duller than the star
> That brightens this new day,
> But still occupies our world,
> And reminds us of dismay.
>
> Still, you fly like a butterfly.
> You are open to change.
> You remember the darkness and isolation
> Of the embalming night
> That allowed you
> To flourish into something
> So much more beautiful than yourself.
>
> You soar over the mountains of overthinking,
> Mountains of guilt and dread
> And words left unsaid.

Your wings spread wide
Across the dry sand-dune.
It's a dune that reaches the horizon
With no end in sight,
And you remind yourself
That each day will turn to night.

But the sun will rise,
And we will try again.
You ride the wave of missed opportunity,
Knowing that no matter how rough the tide,
You can rise like a dolphin,
And be struck again by your guiding light.

And as your day comes to an end,
And the night begins to fall,
You can rest easy
Knowing that you survived it all.

You're the warrior of the day—
Gracious for the lessons
That you know will stay.
They will guide you through
The storms of night
Until tomorrow's morning light.

February 12
Day 69

Self lo—What?

I feel so fat. Grotesque. Repulsive. There were so many new clients admitted this week. They probably think I'm disgusting. I want to cry so badly right now. I used to be skinny. They all probably think I am a pig. Why did I allow myself to lose control of my body? How did I manage to gain so much weight? Where did it all come from?!

Fat. Ugly. Disgusting. Failure.

Fat. Ugly. Disgusting. Failure.

Fat. Ugly. Disgusting. Failure.

You know, it's funny. Sometimes, when you say a word too often, it begins to lose its meaning. Yet, the more I reiterate this negative self-talk, the more it echoes through my ears—like a ghost in an abandoned hall.

Valentine's Day is coming up.

Why can't I just love myself?

February 13

Day 70

How am I supposed to look at food as the opposite of the enemy, when all it does is make me gain weight

FEBRUARY THIRTEEN TWO THOUSAND 8TEEN

Let that shit go

February 14
Day 71

Lent.

As today is the first day of Lent, I become reminded of all of the years I spent these preceding 40 days giving up those things which I loved most. Whether it be chocolate or social media, I utilized these next 40 days to shape myself into (what I perceived to be) a better version of myself. I found it so necessary to deprive myself, restrict myself, and prioritize self-judgment and self-comparison.

What better way than to begin this Easter season than on Valentine's Day—a day that serves as a reminder of love. It is a reminder for us to practice warmth, compassion, and empathy towards others. It is a reminder of God's everlasting love for us, and a reminder of the love He wishes that we would just share with ourselves. Instead of using this Lenten season to fast from your favorite food or pastime, utilize this time to fast from hurtful words. Fast from selfishness and bitterness. Fast from grudges and worry. It is by shying away from that which brings us pain, as opposed to those things that bring us joy, that will allow us to transform into the most beautiful versions of ourselves.

February 15
Day 72

Dear Eating Disorder,

It's been a long journey together. We've been through some ups and downs, some highs and lows, and some happies and some crappies. Listen, I'm tired. You've taken everything out of me: my love for school, for friends, for participation in clubs and social outings. You have filled my mind with thoughts of bitterness and self-loathing, and of disgust and judgment. I will never be able to understand why you thrive off of eliciting sadness from others. How do you find bliss in suffering? How could you possibly be someone I would ever associate myself with?

In short, it's not me, it's *you*.

February 16
Day 73

Rise
Against
All
Odds.

February 17
Day 74

Johanna.

There were just the two of us in treatment today. I haven't had a great opportunity to get to know Johanna. She, myself, and the therapist walked into the group room to begin a session on positive social media, and society's blemishes. I curled up into a ball on the L-shaped couch, practicing the grounding acts I've heard time and time again from my therapists.

"Visualize 5 things:" I thought. "1. The walls". They are not white enough to make this place look like an insane asylum, but not taupe enough to provide the homey essence they were going for. I wonder whose job it is to pick out the paint colors for each treatment room.

I'm curious as to whether or not they found themselves standing in Aisle 4 of Home Depot. If, while browsing the wall of samples, they would have wondered what would occur in the room to be painted. Would they know the pain that piled pounds on each emaciated patient, who walked through the milieu? Would they know the shrieks and sobs that would echo through these rooms? It's a sadness that no noise-machine could wash away.

Maybe the walls were white when they were first painted. Maybe they were crisp, and light, and pure. Maybe the weight of hostility and depression aged them. Maybe they were stained with the filth of our distortions, our past, and our self-criticisms. I always thought tears were clear, but maybe they are as dirty as our fears.

February 18
Day 75

Skies.

When I was in high school,
I used to go to dance classes.
Super stereotypical.
It was a muse that allowed
All of my problems
To fade away.

However,
When I'd leave the studio,
I'd be overcome with a wave of reality,
As my eyes met each day's beautiful sunset.
Every night,
I would take pictures
Of the brightness of the sky
And the beauty of the clouds.

In art class,
When given independent projects,
I would steer away
From still-lifes and self-portraits,
In order to paint the prettiest sunset
I could imagine.

One day,
Someone asked me why I loved the sunset so much,
And I responded:
"He always told me that he loved my eyes,

because they were like windows to the soul.

    Well, the sky is my window to the
    universe.

When you look into someone's eyes,
you see that there is so much more to that
person.

    A much deeper layer.

The sky is a reminder that there is so much
more to life.

    More than my failed English grades,
    Or the size of my jeans,
    Or his new girlfriend, whose eyes are so
    much prettier than mine".

"Life is a mural you create. Every action you take is just a

BRUSH STROKE

LIFE IS ASX wonderful as you make it

MAKE YOURS BEAUTIFUL.

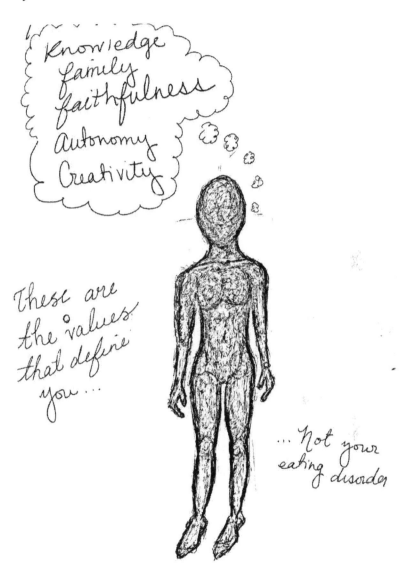

Knowledge
family
faithfulness
Autonomy
Creativity

These are
the values
that define
you ...

... Not your
eating disorder

February 22
Day 79

Dinner.

Isolation from worldly distractions—that's how I would describe dinners at TFC. Every night, we sit at the long dining room table with our varying meals. Each one of us too nervous to raise our eyes from our plates—in fear of judgment of the macronutrients and calories and self-consciousness. We're encouraged to remain mindful. We are prompted to become cognizant of the texture of our foods; the flavor of our foods; the experience we have whilst eating.

Throughout the meal, we are to leave our phones in our bags. We cannot read, or draw, or twiddle our thumbs. It is just us, the food, and the rare flutter of light-hearted conversation. The idea of this is to minimize distractions. We are encouraged to remain present, grounded, and to not fall victim to the anxieties that cause our minds to wander.

Have you ever been forced to eat when you didn't want to? Imagine those days when you would stay home sick from school. You'd have a sore throat, and all you would want to do is fold yourself in a blanket, and sleep. The thought of swallowing anything... the pain that it would bring... the discomfort... You're entirely averted to meals. Your mom would make you anything—soup, milkshakes—anything just to get calories in. That's how my life has been for the past few months. I've lived my life with a sore throat, without a doctors note.

122

Throughout the remainder of our time in treatment, we are asked to remain off of our devices— allowing ourselves to explore the feelings and emotions that we once used fasting to numb away. It is miserable. Starving oneself is painful, but coming face-to-face with the emotions and realities that you have pushed off for so long is another kind of hell. However, opening oneself to his/her inner demons, and embracing the flaws and imperfections of one's life is the first step in whole-hearted living.

Without periods of self-reflection, it can be impossible to discover your true potential, capabilities, and aspirations aside from just skating by in life. The idea that we have the freedom to tackle the unimaginable is a scary concept. Becoming an extraordinary person is a big responsibility.

Growing up, we are encouraged to be extraordinary, but we may fall comfortable in the warm and tranquil state of living an ordinary life. It is through overcoming these fears and allowing yourself to become vulnerable to the harsh realities of life, that we may begin to flourish.

February 23
Day 80

Things to do when all else seems pointless:

- [ ] Go on a bike ride
- [ ] Find a hiking trail
- [ ] Try a new Pinterest recipe
- [ ] Make new door decorations
- [ ] Make someone a birthday card
- [ ] Draw a Mandala
- [ ] Play a record
- [ ] Light a candle
- [ ] Take the train into the city
- [ ] Plan your future
- [ ] Watch a movie
- [ ] Go to a pet shop and play with some puppies
- [ ] Find a pottery studio and sign up for a class
- [ ] Do yoga
- [ ] Find a Groupon for a massage
- [ ] Meal prep for tomorrow
- [ ] Play *Disney Sing It* with your roommates
- [ ] Call mom

February 24
Day 81

Ethan Dodds.

He was the first person to make me feel beautiful. The first one to comfort me when I felt self-conscious. He normalized my ideations of obtaining the perfect body, and preparing the perfect meals. He encouraged my vigorous calorie counting and hours of exercise. He was there for me when I was alone. Ethan Dodds found me at my weakest.

February 25
Day 82

"If you want to work on your art, then work on your life"

I often find that I look for beauty in the most materialistic things. Be it having the perfect Instagram feed, or fitting into certain sized jeans, or trying to find meaning in the most minuscule conversations...I get fixated on finding a purpose. In reality, art, or appearances, is not something that should be correlated with beauty. I'm sure that each and every one of us has gone to an art museum, or seen a painting and said: "What the heck is that?"

It's okay that you don't find each painting, sculpture, or inch of your body to be congruent with societies constructs of "beautiful". Art isn't supposed to be beautiful. Art is supposed to make you feel something. Not every moment in our lives is shaped like the highlight-reel we mold on social media. But, each moment of our lives should elicit a feeling. Each moment should shape us into better versions of ourselves.

Life wasn't meant to be lived boringly. We all have these amazing quirks, and spontaneous interactions, that shape our beautiful souls. Why would you want to take that away, and blend in with the wall? You are destined to be so much more than another coat of paint. Make yourself your own. You're a damn work of art...

February 26
Day 83

2am

My favorite time to talk to people
Is at two in the morning.
At 2am, the only thing you are concerned with
Is sleeping.
You're not preoccupied
With what you look like,
Or about impressing anyone with your mindless banter.

You are selfish.
All you want to do is sleep.
You have not a single care in the world.

Your focus rests solely
On the cool bursts of air
That brush your face
When you sink your head
Into your pillow.

You're drawn to the ticklishness of your eyelashes
As opposed to the closeness of your thighs.

Those words that leave your mouth
Are thoughtless
And wonderful
And filled with your mind's
Most subconscious requests.

At two in the morning,
It is the conversations
That I have with you
That unveil your true being.

You experience a being who is not overcome
By societal norms
Or anxieties
Or masks.
At two in the morning,
You are bare.

February 27
Day 84

Mirror Work.

This afternoon, a therapist at TFC asked me to close my eyes. She took my hand and guided me across the milieu, and asked me to open my eyes. Gazing ahead, standing in front of the bathroom mirror, we took a long hard stare. As juvenile as it may seem, and despite how I cover it up with all of my infamous "mirror selfies", my reflection is something I've refused to accept.

She asked me to look at myself directly in the eye and describe what I saw. Reduced to tears, I was at a loss for words. In a moment like that, what would you say to a body that you've spent so much time at war with?

"Beauty is what I see." She said.

With that, I understood that she was not talking about the standard, aesthetically-pleasing, beauty. For beauty isn't found in the eyes, swollen from crying, nor in tension headaches from overthinking. Beauty isn't found in the pain in your chest after screaming, nor is it found in self-loathing. There is nothing glamorous about craving a sleep in which you don't want to wake up. It isn't beautiful to constantly feel as if everyone hates you, and that you're a burden to everyone you meet. It isn't beautiful to lose motivation for things you once loved— letting them collect dust while you feel yourself slowly crack into pieces.

At times, life isn't fair, and it is most certainly not beautiful. But getting through it. Recovering. Healing. Those happenings are absolutely stunning. The realization that you laughed more than you cried that day; when the slightest bit of happiness you can feel is fighting its way out of that dark cloud. Picking up the old hobbies you spent hours doing, or feeling motivated to go outside and even get out of bed—it's relieving. Feeling yourself slowly climb up the deep, dark hole you were stuck in for so long; actually taking the time to realize that you are worthy of that little bit of happiness; having those smiles you felt like you'd never have again—that's one of the most beautiful things in the world. That is true beauty. I hope you can look at yourselves in the mirror before bed tonight. Truly see yourself, and revel in the beauty of your being.

February 28
Day 85

Geez.

Johanna hasn't been in treatment for the last few weeks. Some of the clients have been saying that she was caught shooting up heroin in her car, during one of our breaks. Nice.

MARCH

IN LIKE A LION
OUT LIKE A BEAST

I don't understand. I feel like I have no feeling...

March 2
Day 87

Pizza.

A client named Ryan started here a few weeks ago. She's become one of my best, most supportive friends. She's one of those people that make you remember what it's like to be happy. She makes you laugh so hard that you can't remember what it felt like to never want to smile again. She just came back from an internship in Florida. I sat next to her in our groups, and asked her about it. It must be nice, I thought—to be able to soak up the summer sun all year round; to be happy.

We have restaurant night tonight, and I want to cry. It's pizza.

I used to have a dog named Leroy. We adopted him when I was 13. I was at a sleepover at the time, when my mom called me. She told me that she had just left our house, to come to pick me up. "Oh," she added, "and we have a surprise for you". When my mom pulled up in her red 4x4, my siblings and dad were sitting anxiously alongside her. Before I knew it, we sped down the turnpike in anticipation. We approached this beautiful suburban house, and before we got the chance to place our feet on the freshly cut grass, Leroy escaped the gates of the central Long Island Colonial. He greeted my 3-year-old sister with enough kisses to never make her question if love exists, ever again.

My dog started getting sick in September. I was back at school. He was a good boy. It wasn't fair. His favorite food was pizza. I don't eat pizza anymore.

March 3
Day 88

Bruised.

> If what I was feeling right now could be defined in a
> color, it'd be somewhere in between black and blue.

March 4
Day 89

Two Birds.

I woke up one morning, and like any other, I drove myself to treatment. I listened to the latest self-love song on the radio, wondering if the artist even accepted her own words as she sang. When I arrived, I walked into the bathroom, waiting to catch sight of the cliche positive affirmations, which were taped to the mirror. The mirror was bare. I suppose that, the night before, the janitorial staff took them down. It just goes to show life's cruel ability to snatch any glimmer of hope. Further up on the wall is an image of two birds, cuddling their child. "It must be nice," I thought. It must be one of life's most beautiful happenings – to have a child. I remember one affirmation that was mounted on the wall read "treat yourself as you would treat your child". As difficult as that is to face, it becomes more taxing to face this reality when that possibility is taken away.

Amenorrhea is, by far, the least glamorous aspect of an eating disorder. It's an overlooked, shame-provoking taboo, that we need to begin talking about.

I used to say that I never wanted kids. That I wanted to be married to my career, or maybe my disorder. I found sufficiency in materialism and simplicity. Anorexia took away more than my sense of happiness. At age 20, it gave me the bone mineral density of someone in their 60s. It took away my prospects for a normal, future life. Not only did I hate my body's aesthetics, but now, for I hated it for its functionality.

And with that thought, it happened. I got my period back. It has been 13 months, and the body that I have dragged through the gates of hell was finally forgiving me for the era of abuse. There is a life beyond anorexia that is awaiting me. There is a beauty and a light that is still within me. This vessel, which has been docked for so long, is ready to set sail once again. It is ready for the tides of triumph and tribulation.

March 5
Day 90

I wonder.

  Sometimes I wonder if I am worthless.

  I wonder if I have a reason.

  I wonder if I have a purpose.

  I wonder if God has a plan for me,

  Or if I am just a test-run.

  Why should I find meaning and value in this life,

  Which I have forced myself to shrink within?

March 6

Day 91

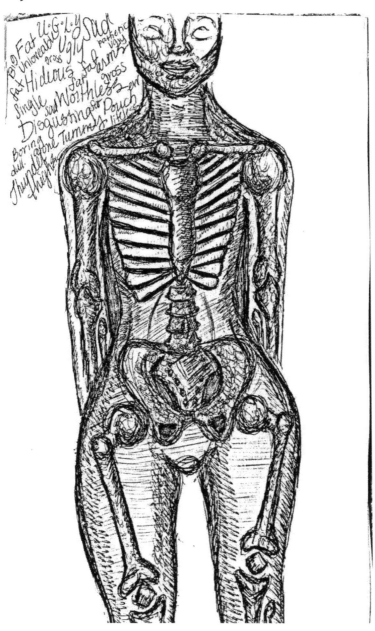

March 7

Day 92

feeling	soul craving	soul feeding
sadness	comfort	get a hug; call Connor; watch comedy show
anxiety	stability	take a walk; exercise; scream
guilt	reassurance	comfort, positivity & call people
shame	validation	have someone listen to you
loneliness	support & love & comfort	research; call someone; play games
happiness	spread fullness	do kind acts

S T O P

stop; take a step back; observe the situation; proceed mindfully

March 8
Day 93

Space Travel.

On Tuesday, I was in my Exercise Physiology Lab, and we were participating in a body composition assessment. I had come to the lab with so much anxiety— preparing to finally see myself as the grotesque image I display to others. I went back and forth over whether to participate. I could hear ED craving the attention of the evaluation, while my healthy brain simultaneously wanted to just take part in the activity, like a normal person. So, I did it. I prepared to step into the bodpod, but first, we had to step on the scale. I was in just a sports bra, spandex shorts, and a swimmers cap, yet, when the professor asked me to step on the scale, I still braced my stomach. It was as if trying to flex any musculature would alter my gravitational pull to the ground. I felt as if I was on The Biggest Loser. I was awaiting the suspenseful and shocking and shameful weight results. I'll get to how I reacted to the number in a second.

Stepping into the bodpod felt like walking into a spaceship. With gushing air compressing against every notch and contour of my skin, I managed to stay as still as possible. I allowed my thoughts to fly away with the breeze that draped my density. For that brief moment in time, there was silence. Peace, even. I imagined I was being shuttled away to a distant world, where the only thought that would preoccupy my mind would be the splendor of the stars floating in the vast beyond.

I was abruptly awoken from this daydream by the sound of the air seal unlocking. And, at that moment, it all seemed like nothing at all. It was just an experiment. I saw my data light up on the computer monitor, adjacent to the bodpod. My weight, body fat percentage, muscle mass percentage, and bone-mineral density was displayed on the screen, and I was okay with what I saw! I recognized that these numbers are just numbers. They are just my physiological data.

The number that presents itself on the digital clock is just a few pixels being illuminated by electricity. They don't define me! This is crazy! Is this what it feels like to be normal?! To see your weight and body and feel indifferent? Maybe the bodpod machine actually did transport me to another world.

March 9
Day 94

"Therapist Wanted".

       If I consider Diane's point of view, I guess I would have a hard time understanding where my doubts and fears are coming from. Hell, I don't even know where they derive from. I'm so headstrong, and stubborn. I think I'm the total opposite of her organized manifestation. And with that being said, I just don't understand how someone so different from me is going to be able to pull me out of this. She and I haven't been getting along lately. Our sessions are painful. It's like conversing with someone for hours on end, but never being able to break through the confines of small talk. I question if she even knows a thing about me. Can you blame me for feeling so alone all the time?

       Anyway, Ryan told me that I should apply for the same internship that she worked for. She said that I'd be good at it. I sent them my resume yesterday. I don't really know what they could possibly see in me. I don't even know why I bothered. I don't know, we'll see. What's the worst that could happen?

March 10
Day 95

"The only person you should try to be better than, is the person you were yesterday."

- *Matty Mullins*

Feeling numb all of the time just sucks. I feel like I am really on a downward slope. I am at TFC six days a week. I'm seeing an outpatient therapist, nutritionist, and psychiatrist once a week. We're at day 95 of intensive treatment. I just feel like an absolute failure. Shouldn't I be getting better by now?

They say I should "Just take it day by day... hour by hour if need be". Well, I don't know how much longer I'll have the patience for it. Reaching for a light in a dark tunnel is exhausting. It's like seeing the most beautiful blouse on the highest shelf, and being too short to reach it.

I look at my painfully happy friends for reference, sometimes. I don't admire their emotions out of jealousy, but out of curiosity. I'm finding it harder and harder to remember the last time I was genuinely happy. Actually, scratch that. The last time I was wholeheartedly happy was my 20th birthday. I just felt so loved and so beautiful. I didn't feel guilty, feel the need to restrict myself, or feel the need to bite my tongue. I relish myself. I relish my former self. I wish that was my last memory.

I am beginning to feel like this "hour by hour" thing is becoming a "minute by minute" thing.

March 11
Day 96

I crave a body as outwardly terrifying as my inner demons.

I feel fat. And overweight. And huge. How did I allow myself to eat tonight? I'm such a failure. How did I allow this to happen? I just want to be happy. I just want to go home. I hate my body. I'm disgusting. I yearn for my hip bones and my spine and my pointy acromions. Sunken eyes and protruding cheekbones. Emaciated wrists and razor blade collarbones.

March 12
Day 97

Jenga.

As good as this day has been, I feel a little bit off. Shouldn't I feel happy? Lively? Enthralled, even? It has been a good day so far. It's been normal, which is all I could ever ask for. I should be feeling something. Instead, I find myself feeling numb again. I almost feel like a Jenga tower. When you remove a level's side bricks, and the weight of the tower is resting on a single brick...and the size of the brick pales in comparison to the remainder of the tower...

...And while the brick is minuscule in scale to its burden, it's strength could move (or more literally, hold) a mountain. Maybe this feeling is a testament to my defense mechanisms? Maybe my body, or my mind, is too scared to reap the benefits of happiness? It's been so long since I've experienced joy. I'm so scared that someone is going to say something, or look at me the wrong way, or maybe the wind will blow in a certain direction, and I'll just snap. It's moments like this that I crave the feeling of hunger. Is it comfortable? *No.* Is it pleasant? *No.* I don't know what it is, but it's something. It's something that reminds me that I'm still here.

Freshman year, I never went to bed in a bad mood. A smile, that stretched from ear to ear, was plastered on my face. Each night, my vision grew blurry with the tears that filled my eyes from laughing. I read somewhere that laughing for seven minutes each day can extend your life. I used to think I'd live to be 105. Now, I wonder how many years I've lost because of the turmoil my brain is enduring.

March 13
Day 98

It is what it is.

Everyone keeps telling me: if it's meant to be, it will happen. I don't know if I believe that. That has never been the case for me. I thought results came from hard work. I thought results came from determination. I thought results came from desire-motivated action.

I can't live my life *hoping* that it all comes together and works out. I can't. I need endless perseverance to get through this.

March 14

Day 99

I don't really have much to say today.

    Mentally,

        I'm exhausted. The thoughts that run around my
        mind in circles leave me winded.

    Physically,

        I'm longing for a sensation other than this
        isolating numbness.

    Emotionally,

        I'm curious if I even have emotions other than
        sadness anymore.

    Socially,

        I crave the understanding of another. The
        validation that I am not enduring this hell alone.

    Spiritually,

        I pray that God will save even my worst enemies
        from the possibility of grappling with this reality.

March 15

Day 100

alter your world
sentimental
kind
sound
JOY
NEW
you will
be found
just
be
REAL
Simple
PURE
adore
goodness,
embark
you are more than
who you see
sweet
value
simply
I am what I make up
dear
sound
right
what
Everything you need,
your courage, strength
compassion and love;
everything you need is
already within you.
delight
Pretty
cherish
we
love

March Fifteen 2018

March 16
Day 101

Things I learned today:

- Boundaries are how we teach others how to treat us.
- It takes true strength to know your needs.
- If I ask for something (e.g. help) in a polite, reasonable fashion, people will not be mad at me.
- How can you care for others, if you cannot care for yourself?
- If I cannot fix something myself, that does not make me inadequate. Why else would God have given us 7 billion neighbors? That's 14 billion helping hands.
- You can't read minds.

March 17
Day 102

Beautiful?

Someone called me "beautiful" today, and I laughed. I think the part of self-love that I struggle with the most, is my worthiness of it all. I'm a horrible, selfish person. I cannot see the parts of myself that are worthy of love. I far too easily find a "but".

Does a homeless man feel like the richest man alive after finding a $10 bill on the street? I don't imagine so. How, then, could one receive a compliment in the midst of self-loathing, and be expected to become engrossed in self-love and compassion? That's a lot to ask.

March 18
Day 103

In the midst of my inappropriate reaction to Chinese Food:
        I just met with Giselle, the new dietician. I was in
our Intuitive Eating group, and I was having a panic attack
over the Chinese food we are supposed to be having at
our restaurant outing tonight. I figured that by sharing my
anxieties with someone, I would be able to stay
accountable for completing my meals. Against the wishes
of ED, I shared with her my physical symptoms of
anxiety. How I was shaking. How my heart was racing.
How I just wanted to crawl out of my skin and hide. She
then asked me to go into detail about how my compliance
has been going. I lied. I told her I was completing 100%.

        She gave me a long stare, and told me that she
knew I wasn't being honest. She told me that my weight
was plummeting again. Oh no. They can't think that
something is wrong with me again. I want to sustain this.
No more losing weight. Just until I get out. I can't
breathe. I want to be happy, but I know I shouldn't be.
Just breathe. You don't have to eat. You're not hungry.
Breathe. Show your self-control. Believe in yourself.

        Okay so instead of eating dinner tonight I can
watch a movie, learn a new song on my guitar, maybe go
to bed early, go on a long walk…This will be okay. I'm
not hungry. I'm not hungry. I can't stop thinking about
my arms and my stomach and my thighs and my
chipmunk cheeks. All of the other clients must think I'm
so fat. They probably don't even think I'm sick. I'm so
embarrassed. I'm so ashamed of myself.

March 19
Day 104

Just trying to process this.
    I'm having really strong urges right now. I want to restrict. I want to give in to the voices in my head. I want to be numb. I just have a lot of pain inside of me right now. I've been trying to write, and draw, and use all of these coping skills, but nothing is working. This is the type of fluttering in your chest that you need a good cry to get rid of. How am I supposed to be happy when my heart is screaming?

March 20

Day 105

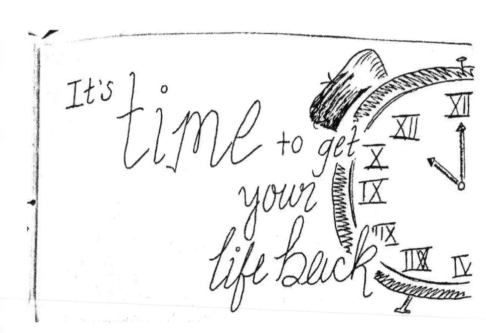

March 21

Things I'm Grateful For:

1. Fuzzy socks.
2. Listening to old voicemails.
3. The first watermelon of the summer season.
4. Matching shampoo and conditioner sets.
5. Matching luggage sets.
6. Finishing an essay before it's due, and getting to spend the rest of your night deciding which Netflix series to start.
7. Making art.
8. That moment when you though you forgot to bring a pen to class, and you hopelessly look in your backpack for one, and you miraculously come across one, by the grace of God.
9. Flowers.
10. The look of asphalt after it rains.

March 22
Day 107

Dear Kylie,

     I wanted to write you this letter in case you ever forgot how wonderful you are. Truly. Even though we are years and miles apart, I look up to you. You are *my* role model. You treat people with kindness. You treat them as kindly as you would like to be treated. If someone snaps at you, or is rude to you, you have this amazing capacity to brush it off.

     You uphold this stature, as if nothing at all has happened. You are resilient. No matter how mean people may be, or as jealous as some people may seem, I never want you to forget how truly beautiful you are. You have a smile that can light up the darkest room. You have a laugh that would make those stone-faced British security guards crack a smile. You are the most talented person I know. Whether it is dancing, or drawing, or just giving friendly advice, you do everything with love and passion. Never lose that. That spark is what transforms you from an ordinary girl, into an extraordinary young woman.

I love you,
Your Sister

March 23
Day 108

Lots and Lots and Lots of Thoughts.

So we are sitting here in our process group. Diane is running the session, so naturally, no one is talking. No one has anything they want to share around her. Instead of actually speaking to us (you know, like a mental health professional), she told us to just journal about our feelings instead. So, here I am to tell the tale.

So Kirsten? What are you bottling up? Hmmm. Maybe the fact that, when we watched *Mona Lisa Smile* in our Body Acceptance group, I was too distracted by trying to guess the weights of all of the actresses to even pay attention to the plot. I wish I had their collarbones, and chiseled cheekbones, and pursed red lips. I wonder how it must feel for Diane... to sit here amongst client silence.

After treatment on Tuesday, mom called me on her way home. She told me about how upset dad is. How, sometimes, he feels like no one cares about him. How he sometimes feels like he doesn't matter. I wonder if he knows that I feel the same way most of the time.

Dear God,

Please provide me with the wisdom to understand exactly what my father needs right now. I would sacrifice anything to allow him to sustain a more healthy mind, body, and spirit. No one deserves this hell.

March 24
Day 109

*My dearest **E**than **D**odds,*

There comes a point when you have to move on in life. You have to turn the page, and move on to the next chapter. With that in mind, I always knew that the healthiest relationships are the ones that are perfectly balanced. 50/50. Like a level teeter-totter.

My dearest *E*than *D*odds, over the last few months, I've been feeling as if our relationship has been more 80/20. I feel like I give you all of me... everything I have to offer the world. I've been trying my absolute best to be everything that you could possibly want. And, for the last few weeks, I have been trying to plan my future. I have been searching for, and anticipating, things to look forward to—summer, a possibility of the internship, grad school, happiness. At the end of the day, I've come to a realization.

My dearest *E*than *D*odds, there are only so many hours in the day. And, with all that I have planned for my life, there is just not enough time for me to give you what you want. If I feel this way now, I can't even imagine how hard it would be to reinitiate this break-up after further months of continuous heartache and destructive habits. You put me on the backburner. I'm not okay. I know that I am so much more valuable than the way you make me feel. I worked endlessly for you. I spent too many gruelling months fighting for perfection. I know how it feels to fight for something you truly want, and have all efforts be futile.

Now, you can either agree with me, or disagree with me. You can attempt to prove me wrong, but this is it. I'm moving on with my life. And I just don't understand how we could possibly continue this relationship if you're not willing to be there for me. Right here. Right now. I shouldn't have to look a certain way to get the love and support I need. You should be able to see that.

I have loved you,

KC

March 25
Day 110

I didn't think I had anything to look forward to in life anymore. I didn't think I had a purpose to serve. What could I possibly have to offer this world? The voices in my head had silenced me for so long. What if, when I finally learned to speak up again, I would have nothing to say? Nothing that would speak truer than the slander I abused myself with.

I heard back from the Internship. They hired me.

When going through really dark times, you may find yourself conforming to an "end game"—this preconceived notion that, maybe, anything other than misery just isn't in the cards for you.

You begin to settle—for less life, less love, less fulfillment.

I didn't think I had anything to look forward to in life anymore. I thought all of my dreams were a bust. I lost all motivation for all of the things that I loved… the things that I found passion in… the things that made my heart sing…

I stopped dancing. I stopped singing. I stopped laughing.

What did it even matter anymore? What was the point?

But God works in mysterious ways, and I will never, ever again underestimate His power, nor His plan.

If I had never gotten sick... I would have never been admitted to TFC.

If I had never been admitted to TFC... I would have never met Ryan.

If I never met Ryan... I would have never found a reason to believe in myself. I was lost.

If I had never lost myself...
... I would not have learned how to find myself. I would have never learned that there is always a light to be found if you open your eyes in the right direction. Even if it is just a glimmer, any amount of light makes your world a little less dark.

Through all of the rubble, I found a diamond. Through pain-staking hours of sadness, I've found something to look forward to. Through all the pain and suffering and disappointments and rejections, maybe there *is* a destiny awaiting us that is so much greater than any of us know. Maybe there *is* a path paved for us.

Maybe things *do* happen for a reason.

March 26
Day 111

March 27
Day 112

March 28
Day 113

I'm so depressed today.
      I am so sad. So lethargic. I don't want to be here. I don't want to be anywhere. I am numb. There is no substance, or feeling, or depth. I've failed. Loneliness has a funny way of making your mind run wild with all kinds of voices. Sitting here, I find myself writing, and opening up, and exploring myself. Still, I don't understand how I could feel so alone. I guess that loneliness comes when you don't know your worth. Who'd want to get to know a brick wall, anyway?

March 29
Day 114

I'm trying to try.

We're sitting here in our Body Acceptance group
listening to *Try* by Colbie Caillat. I just had a session with
Diane where I broke down. I started crying and screaming
at her. I have never lashed out like that before. She just
doesn't care about me. She doesn't know anything about
me. Maybe if she did her job, I wouldn't be in treatment
anymore. I've been here for more than 3 months and I'm
in the same place as I was before. Except fatter.

My eating disorder is so manipulative. It finds joy in
suffering and sadness. It finds success through accolades as
opposed to development.

I hate it. I hate her. I hate this place. I hate myself. I hate
my body. I hate the world. Why is this happening to me?!
What did I do to deserve this?! What bad karma did I put
out into the universe that brought this upon me?!

March 30
Day 115

Ugh.

Giselle just met with me, and she is concerned. She just
wants me to love myself and it just breaks her heart to see
how much I'm fighting and struggling. I can't really
remember what else we talked about, because I couldn't
stop hating myself for being hungry for dinner.

March 31
Day 116

Hmm.

Am I feeling this angry and frustrated because I'm not eating again?

APRIL

APRIL SHOWERS BRING
LIGHTNING AND THUNDER

April 1
Day 117

Easter Prayer

As the sun begins to set
On this dismal day,
They gather together in silence
And begin to pray.

The shrill and somber sobs
Echo through the hall,
And as their dreams fell victim
To worry, they bawled.

From these kids who awaited
The splendor and joy
Of a brand new day,
And new Easter toy,

To the crippled clients
Who creep, cry, and crawl
along this cursed life
That burdens them all.

A burden as heavy
As their weary hearts haul.
Oh Lord, Almighty God,
Please grace them with gall.

As You did with Your Son,
When He answered Your call.

You helped bear His cross,
And carried Him with each fall.

As the sun rises high,
Their spirits fall awol.
And on this Easter morning,
Please remember them all.

The filth of their tears
Are not desolate and clear.
They, instead, stain dark
And reek of sheer fear.

Lord grant them today
Your mercy and call,
As You gather here now
To protect us all.

April 2
Day 118

The Sound of It All

    It's a room filled with the most interesting speakers
    All using different tongues.
    It's being invited to a jubilant feast
    With your mouth sewn shut.
    It's like walking into an art museum
    When you've been blinded by the sun.
    It's hot and blistering and oh-so crowded
    Yet, you're the only one.

    It's the cry of destruction
    Reverbing in your mind.
    While you can't stop
    Replaying the thoughts:

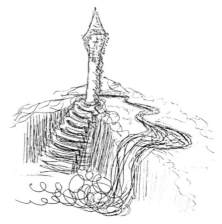

    Rewind. Play. Pause.
    Rewind. Play. Pause.
    Rewind. Play. Pause.
    Rewind. Pause. Stop.

    You stop yourself from
    releasing
    The pain you have inside.
    For they're guarded by those inner beasts
    Who steal and swell and brine.
    You're trapped within that tall brick tower,
    As you fester up inside,
    The hopes and dreams of your knight in armor,
    From a kingdom far and wide.

April 3
Day 119

I feel shame in my heart.

It feels like a thick, lead brick being pumped through each fragile vessel. It's like that heart-sunken feeling when you walk into a room of people that know your deepest, darkest secret. It feels like somebody tied up my aorta— knotting it together like brand-new shoelaces. It feels like I'm being transfused with abrasive stones and pebbles.

It feels like carrying the weight of the world on the back of your neck, when all you asked for was a break. It's the burning sensation of getting soapy water in your eyes, with the shampoo that promised you that you'd be without a tear.

It tastes like spoiled tomato sauce.

Or rotten milk.

Or like that meal, which you can't bring yourself to eat.

April 4
Day 120

I'm in such a bad mood.

Of course, our restaurant outing is Chinese. Again. It's like this is a joke. I want to cry. I am so upset. I refuse to eat dinner tonight. I'll do something. Anything. I'll make those 30 minutes fly by. I am going to have a nervous breakdown, and start to cry. I don't want to eat. I'm not going to. I'm not going to. I'm not going to. I'm not going to. Why am I crying? Stop crying. I'm embarrassing myself. I can't do this. Everyone's looking at me. Everyone's wondering why I'm such a baby. How did I become so fat? I feel like a cow, or maybe a pig, or some other caged animal. No wonder people don't want to be around me. Who would want to be around someone like this? Who would want to be around someone that looks like me, or feels the way I do all the time? I'm toxic. I don't even deserve to be here. If I eat dinner, I'm going to gain weight. I feel so worthless. I feel so huge. There's an elephant sitting on my chest. I can't breathe. I just want to cry some more. I can't do this. I'm so scared. I can't expand anymore. I can't. I can't. I can't. I can't do this. I need to talk to Giselle, but she doesn't care. She doesn't care, because I'm too fat to have an eating disorder. I just need to get over myself. I can't live like this. I cant live in this body. I can't do this. People here probably only like me because I'm fat and it makes them feel better. I can't do this anymore.

April 5
Day 121

Time.

I wasted so much time.
I spent 6 agonizing months
Attempting to achieve
A nonexisting perfection.

I starved.
I isolated.
I hurt myself.

All this, so that I can return to my fat, annoying, loner
excuse of a person.

April 6
Day 122

Pros of recovery
◊ you can actually smile again
◊ your hands are no longer freezing
◊ for second servings of Krave without guilt

"Every great story on the planet happened when someone decided not to give up, but kept going no matter what."

"Tough times never last, but tough people do."

April 7
Day 123

Note to self: Be good to yourself and know that you are loved.

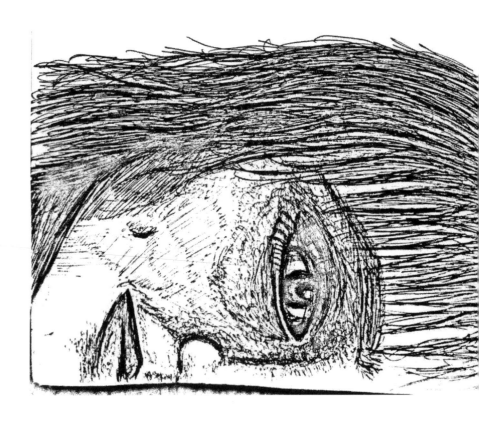

April 8
Day 124

The Box

Lost are the days
Where my mind swells
With thoughts of wonder
Over the miraculous nature
Of a life not lived.

An empty box
Is still a box.

It is a box that can be filled
With anything imaginable.
But be cautious,
For just as a box may be filled
With flowers and awe,
It may just as quickly be embroidered
With jealousy,
Disgust,
And shame.

It can be sewn so meticulously
With a thread of regret,
And hatred can be
Just as easily
Woven through the seams of each crevice.

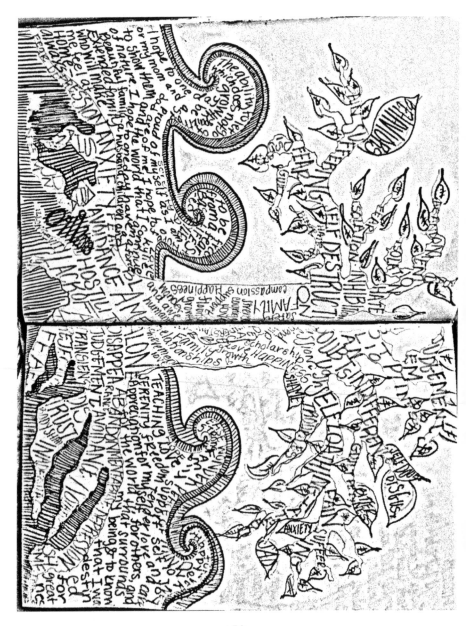

April 10
Day 126

April 11
Day 127

The Encounter

In church on Sunday, I had an encounter with God. For a while, I tried to separate myself from the mass. I'd dodge Fr. Rich's conversations, and I would use the hour of silence to daydream about my perfect, fantasy "cheat day". For so long, I was even scared to have communion because... who even knows how many calories are in those wafers?! But today, the gospel was literally made for me to hear. At this point. At this time. I needed it. After communion today, when I returned to the pew to pray, I felt Jesus kneeling beside me. He was on my right. He placed His left hand on my left shoulder. I told Him that I was struggling. That the self-loathing and self-doubt are standing in my way. He let out a sigh, and answered me, "Everything you could ever need is before you. You have the strength within you. Right now, you are exactly where you need to be. I am carrying you through the darkness, and I will be with you every step of the way". And with that, I opened my eyes and continued with the motions of mass.

Father Rich stopped me on my way out of the mass. He asked if I had a few moments to spare, and I nodded my head. With that, he led my family into the sacristy. He asked me to sit. The cushioned leather felt much better on my hips and spine than the hard pews had. He asked me to lay my hands, palms up, on my lap. He then anointed my palms and head with oil. Mom and Dad placed their hands on my back and prayed the "Our

180

Father" in my name. Father Rich placed his hand on my head and muttered his own prayer—his own private intentions for me.

When the anointing was over, I experienced this overwhelming sense of peace. A golden, illuminated ribbon was unraveling in my core. It spread itself across my extremities, like a shock. I am so loved. I have so many people rooting for me. I long to find this peace in every aspect of my life. Thank you, God.

April 12
Day 128

Worthy

> I am worthy of love.
> I am worthy of wellness.
> I am worthy of happiness.
> I am worthy of serenity.
> I am worthy of contentment.
> I am worthy of joy.
> I am worthy of self-compassion.

April 13
Day 129

Dancing Queen.

When we were little kids in dance class, we'd spend ages staring at our reflections in the mirror—making funny faces, and having dance-offs with our reflections. We found beauty in each and every aspect of ourselves. We'd spend those hours flaunting the strength of the legs we pointed with. We'd revel in the plumpness of our cheeks as we smiled from ear to ear. Yet, somewhere along the line of job-searching and credit-card managing and adulting, our appreciation, for all that our body can do, turn into dissatisfaction.

There is nothing beautiful in the pain of spending your time picking apart each and every flaw. Nothing. Please know that there is no definitive definition of beautiful. Beauty is in the eye of the beholder. It is not defined by physical attributes, but instead by those things which provide one with a sense of bliss. To me, beauty is when you laugh so

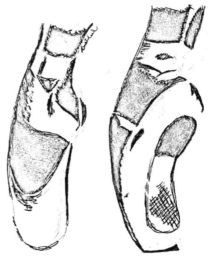

hard that you can't breathe. Beauty is the first warm day of the spring season. Beauty is what you make of it. There are so many better dreams to dream, than for a perfect image. Perfection is an image that society has blinded us from ever seeing within ourselves. Choose to love the funny faces you make; or the way you dance across the floor. Choose to see the beauty of your being.

April 14

Day 130

RayBans

       Eyes as sunken
       As the RayBans that lie
       On the bridge of our noses,
       Too broken to try.

       They're hanging on tight
       To the last bit of hope,
       Before slipping off the edge
       Of that slippery slope.

       We uncovered that
       The parts we most love
       Are the collarbones we hang
       Our heartstrings off of.

       Or the prominences of the bones
       That line our limbs.
       When they blow through the wind,
       They whistle church hymns.

       We trace them like mountainscapes
       That lead us far away
       From this hell on Earth.
       Seldom do we reflect on the way

       Our smiles have the power
       To light up the room.

185

Or how we've learned to flourish
Like flowers in bloom.

Each day, we grow
Inside our minds
And in our hearts
And our spiritual confines.

But, our physical growth
Leaves us to dwell
Over the disgust of a simple
accumulation of cells.

April 15
Day 131

The Ocean.
> I wonder if the ocean ever thinks of itself as just a puddle.
> I wonder if it questions its endlessness.
> I wonder if it believes the coasts that scream
> From miles and miles away.

> Have you ever been told something you don't believe?
> How it sounds like those voices are coming from a distant
> land?

> I don't know.
> Even though I feel as though
> Everyone is talking at me
> From miles away,
> Repetition is the key to memorization.

> Maybe I should just start listening.

April 16
Day 132

My Story

They say that life is a collection of chapters. It is a novel. It's one that is suspenseful, dramatic, adventurous, and moving. We hope that one day, we may play the heroes and heroines in our own little stories. I think it's fair to say that what we want, more than anything, is simply not to become a sad story. I don't think I'll ever be a hero, nor a heroine. I don't think that I'll find the cure to cancer, nor do I think that I'll become the first woman President of the United States. I may be "extraordinarily average"; however, my life will not be a "sad story". I may not touch thousands of people with inspirational, thought-provoking words and actions, but I hope that my presence, and zest for life, may one day ignite fires in the few that surround me every day.

Here's the story I will choose to live:

My story began when I was born in a small town on Long Island. I was raised by two very loving parents who taught me what it truly meant to love, unconditionally. My father used to bring my mother flowers every single week. Their union set the tone for how I saw love. Not only did I fall captivated by the idea of romanticized love, but it also set the tone for how I strive to treat, and be treated by, others. I want everyone to feel as special as my father makes my mother feel. I will have a tremendous capacity for love, and friendship, that will carry and overflow itself into my career.

When I graduate, I aim to help anyone who accepts my outstretched hand. I strive to provide those with the grimmest mindsets with at least one smile every day. I will plant flowers in the souls of those who seem barren. These are my passions, and they will drive me.

I will embrace every single day with as much enthusiasm, love, and light as I can. Everything I do with my life, from my career to my family, will be done with a sense of appreciation, completeness, and fullness.

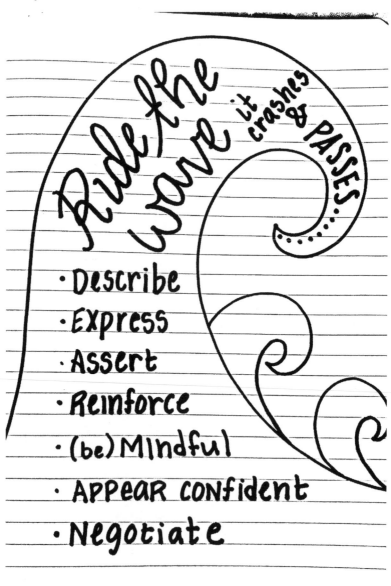

Ride the wave — it crashes & PASSES

- Describe
- Express
- Assert
- Reinforce
- (be) Mindful
- Appear confident
- Negotiate

The only way out of this

hell is through it

Dear Kirstin, ♡ ♡ ♡
you are so beautiful and
strong and worthy of an ED
free life! Keep fighting be
cause you are so worth it!
Love you! Call/text me if you
need anything!!!!

April 20
Day 136

April 21
Day 137

The Hurricane.

Like any other day, I drove myself to TFC. There was supposed to be a storm today, but I didn't expect much. Plus, I walked outside, and there wasn't a drop of precipitation shed from the sky. So, how bad could it be? (Note to self: Never ask yourself: "how bad could it be?")

I noticed that it began to drizzle as I approached the parkway. "Here comes the traffic," I thought to myself, "no one knows how to drive in the rain". Surprisingly, I managed to make it halfway to TFC with ease. Then, boom. Standstill traffic. I was confused as to why my fellow commuters were placing their cars in park. Drivers began leaving their cars to try to catch a glimpse of what was unfolding in the miles ahead.

Slowly, cars began to reverse out of the nearest exits. I couldn't help but laugh. What a sight. It was as if I was rewinding a VHS tape. Easily falling into peer pressure, and without any care of the danger I placed myself in, I followed the carousel through the backstreets of suburban, southern Connecticut.

Every side road I came across during those 45 minutes were dead ends. Collapsed telephone poles and oak trees sailed through the wind. The storm enraged. I couldn't see through my spastic windshield wipers. The trees, which were collapsing left and right, were obstructing the roads. It felt so trying. What was even the point? Why keep trying when all I hit are dead ends?

But, I couldn't just get out of the car and walk away. Especially in the midst of a hurricane, in a dark and scary town that I knew nothing about. I had to shut up and face the music. I had to work, and try new paths. With each failure came a chance to start over and try again. And once I finally came to the road I knew TFC was on, I began to fill with anxiety. What if this final road is blocked? I mean, I'm only 0.2 miles away, but who's to say that there aren't 6 collapsed trees within the next 1,320 feet? I had no other choice. No other avenue or street to turn to. I had to take the plunge, and hope for the best. And if this road would lead me to another dead end, I'd have to pick up my pieces and try again.

Life is filled with countless dead ends,
but there are also sideroads and backroads.
You will find a way out.
Just keep on driving.

April 22
Day 138

Formal

I was in no mood for this night. I had been dreading this night for WEEKS. It was my Spring Formal today, and I didn't want to go. I *really* didn't want to go. At last semester's Fall Formal, I hit my lowest weight. I look back on those pictures with such nostalgia and longing. It just makes me so sad that I've gotten so fat. It makes me just want to curl up in a sweatshirt and hide my hideous body from any eyes, which could ever see me again. How did I hate myself back then? Why did I hate myself back then? I don't even want to know what *October Kirsten* would say to *Now Kirsten*...

I knew that people were going to compare the pictures of me between these past six months. I wanted to cry. I really didn't want to go. But, months ago, I made plans to take Jackson with me. He and I always have so much fun together. He's great. I figured that bringing a date, who makes me feel happy and comfortable, could ease my mind from the intrusive thoughts that surrounded me. It just sucks, you know? I used to love dancing. I used to love getting all dressed up—even if it was for no reason at all. I used to love spending hours with my friends.

So. Here's the thing. When I fell asleep last night, in tears, I prayed to God. I prayed in hopes of having some essence of peace wash over me. "Please," I begged, "please just let me be normal again. Just for one night". I was like Cinderella. I was weeping over this life that fate had found me in. Like her evil stepsisters, my eating disorder had torn every last part of me to shreds. In a jealous rage, my disorder deprived me of everything that could bring me joy in this, seemingly, dismal life.

When I woke up, I may as well have woken up in a glistening blue ballgown, because, for the first time in months, I was happy! A sense of anxiety filled my being, but it wasn't the bad kind! It was the "oh my gosh, today's the last day of school" kind! I was confused at first. I didn't really know what to do with happiness anymore. How are you supposed to react to this? Are you just supposed to sit with it? I don't know, but it was a new lesson I was ready to learn.

When I got out of bed and took that long stare in the mirror, I decided that I was going to do everything in my God-given power to keep this feeling vibrant. I racked my brain for the reasons as to why I had previously been so nervous for this night. I came up with two things:

1. I'm not confident. What if everyone thinks I look fat? What if they think I'm ugly? What if someone says something?
2. I'm scared that no one will want to hang out with me. What if I'm all alone? Who would want to be around someone who doesn't even want to be around herself?

I always do this. I call it "future-tripping". I get so caught up in what I think is going to happen. I spend minutes, on hours, anticipating every possible worst-case-scenario. I talk myself out of doing whatever challenge I was going to present myself with. But, not today, Satan.

I decided to tackle the first point, first. Shocking, right? Anyway, why didn't I feel confident? Was it my dress? The piece was beautiful! It was a slender, cream, v-neck, halter dress with these beautiful red peonies all over the fabric. I love flowers. I used to always love wearing flowery things. "Okay," I thought to myself, "what about this dress makes you feel self-conscious?" Well, this dress is the first article of clothing I've bought since restoring my BMI. It's been really hard for me to step into any stores. I don't want to know what size I've sprouted into. I can't know. I think it would break me.

A few months ago, my best friend, Sara, and I were at the mall. She and I passed by this boutique and caught sight of that beautiful cream dress. She insisted that we go in, and try it on. I was hesitant at first, but agreed. When I came face-to-face with the rack, I didn't want to look at the tags. I was a bit paralyzed, as my eyes scanned the array of numbers. It's funny, as my eyes drew to each greater size, my self-worth deteriorated in direct proportion.

I took a deep breath, and without hesitation, removed my eyes from the rack's trance. I asked Sara if she would pick a few sizes out for me... ones that she believed would fit me. Then, I asked if she would meet me in the dressing room. She handed me each dress, without the labeled clothing hanger. That action still goes down as one of the most self-respecting, assertive things I've ever done for myself, or asked someone to do for me. You know, other than allowing myself to eat again.

When we made it to the dressing room, the very first dress fit like a charm, and without hesitation, I got re-dressed and made a beeline towards the register. Now, looking at the dress that I once found so much beauty in, why am I experiencing a stomach-churning sadness? "I could be wearing Kate Middleton's wedding dress," I thought, "and I'd still think I looked like a garbage can". Instead of following these thoughts down a road of time-wasting self-deprecation, I decided to grab my keys and head to the store. I ended up picking up a new dress. One that I felt GREAT in. One that made me confident. "I can reevaluate the emotions behind the other dress tomorrow. "But right now," I thought, "I just need to focus on being happy".

Next point: Feeling friendless.

"No," I thought, "I'm not going to do this. I am not going to allow these thoughts to embalm me like an unwelcomed hug. I am not going to allow something so dismissive to ring sweet-nothings into my ears."

Other than "future-tripping", one of my favorite mind-corrupting pastimes is "mind-reading". Because, you know, don't we all think we're smart enough to grasp the deepest emotions of others? Like a psychic? Well, again, not today. I do not have the energy to conjure up ideas of what *might* happen. What *might* people say? How *might* people react? What *might* people do?

It's funny. I spent months feeding into (pun intended) this disorder's every whim. I allowed it to consume me (pun intended), in the sole hope of someday being able to scratch the surface of what it means to have a speck of control in your life. Maybe, just maybe, if I fell into the desires of this abusive persona, he'd be able to teach me something about how to lead your life with drive and passion. I don't know if I've ever been so determined to be anything but small.

So, I decided to call my friends. Jackson was already on his drive up, so I'd have him. But, in the meantime, how are my friends supposed to know that I need support when I continue to isolate myself deeper and deeper? So, I called. I allowed the dial tone to drown out the intrusive thoughts. And guess what? They answered. And you know what's even more amazing? They *didn't* hate me for asking for help. They *didn't* think I was needy! They *didn't* think that I was a burden, or some other poor-excuse of a person. Within the hour, Sara, and Georgie, and Bean all came running through my kitchen, and into my room. They donned their most elegant sweatpants. They held their dresses, and their makeup bags, and their smiles.

Something I've learned throughout this journey is that, sometimes, people love being asked for help. While some may find it annoying, others find self-fulfillment in the fact that they can offer a piece of themselves to others. They have tools that can help make a broken soul, whole. And, very often, they just don't know how, or when, it is appropriate to reach out their olive branches.

The night turned out to be amazing. Allowing my friends into the madness of my mind allowed little room for the disorder to creep its tiresome tunes. Jackson, my girlfriends, and I danced the night away. The DJ blasted his music while I blasted out my disordered thoughts. And, just for a moment, I understood what Cinderella must have felt like at the ball.

April 23
Day 139

Numbers.

For as long as I can remember, I've been a numbers person. I found value in comparison of data and tangible values. Whether it be the number on the scale, or the number on the top of an exam; the number of friends I have, or the amount of money in my bank account...it's no wonder why society finds purpose in that which we can measure. In a world so engrossed in competition and societal acceptance, we subject ourselves to toxic relationships and comply with miserable occupations. We do all of this so that we can define ourselves as social and economic elitists. Seldom do we consider the intrinsic, invaluable measurement of our self-worth. In a world obsessed with accolades, take a moment to account for the unique attributes that separate you from the 7 billion other humans on this earth. Comparison is the thief of joy. And this human propensity, to covet the realities of others, is only inflated by the "highlight reels" we all post. Learning to utilize comparison as a motivator of self-love, as opposed to self-destruction, could make the world a more beautiful place.

I want to begin recognizing the kindness shed by another, or the light that they bring into a room. It's a beautiful concept, but it is a difficult task to complete when you're propelled with countless Instagram posts, and Snapchat messages, flaunting the unrealistic. Imagine what life would become if you could elevate your habit of comparison into an art form— if you could isolate those comparisons that leave you miserable, and trade them for juxtapositions that inspire you to make your corner of the world a more wonderful place. Maybe then, we could learn to fall in love with ourselves.

April 24

Day 140

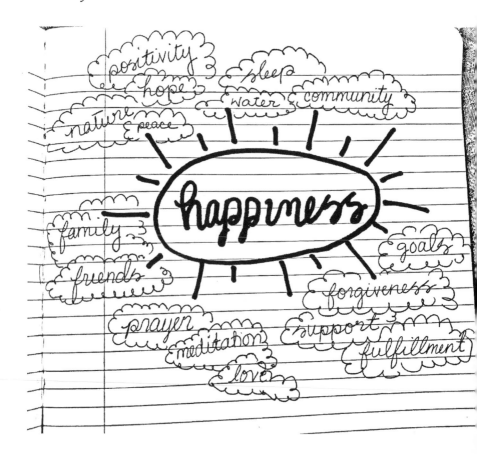

April 25
Day 141

you have so much love in your heart... give some to yourself

the sun will rise & we will try again

April 27
Day 143

They
don't
need to
understand
the process
but they need
to respect the journey.

April 28
Day 144

The sun will rise, and we can try again.

I surrendered to
The dark grey sky,
That loomed overhead
Each passing nigh.

Cries flowed downstream,
Eager to unite.
That way, at least my tears
Wouldn't be lonely tonight.

The breeze was the only
Whisper I could hear,
Other than the echoing
Of my deepest, darkest fears.

But, maybe tomorrow will bring
A shining delight
To the depths of my
Cloudy, stormy night.

May the skies open up.
May the sun shed a ray,
To remind me that there is always some good
In every day.

Sometimes,
I feel like
I'm locked in a
room.
Alone.
No windows,
no skylight.
Just a door
without a knob.

April 30
Day 146

Disposing of further derailment.

As frustrated as I am with Diane, and the argument that we had, it brought me to realize that I cannot look to Diane, or my disorder, to get me out of this abyss. Feeding (pun intended) into these thoughts and behaviors just keeps sending me on an endless loop of self-destruction. To finally beat this disorder, I have to learn to accept myself. I have to learn how to respect myself. Maybe I could learn how to like myself. It just shouldn't be this hard.

MAY

NO RAIN, NO FLOWERS

May 1
Day 147

Morning thoughts.

Today I woke up, reminded that the most selfless decision one can make is to fully participate in life; to shed kindness on this vessel—which carries you along this journey; to channel your frustrations through avenues of self-growth as opposed to self-destruction. Accepting oneself for all of its vulnerability, imperfections, and changes. These bring along wisdom, understanding, and strength. I really urge you to use the final moments of this day of happiness to agree to live a life that is accepting to the help of others. Promise to allow yourself the energy to sustain this life that is deserving of the world. Never settle for less—less life, less joy, or less happiness.

May 2
Day 148

Questions to myself, after pursuing an abusive relationship
with Ethan Dodds:

I wonder what
I'd seen in you,
When life was humble
And blossoms bloomed.

And all was as longing
As the rising sun
For hope, and nourishment,
And some kind of love.

I wonder if your soul
Was ever broken, too.
Have you ever felt like the world
Was entirely against you?

Did you feel loneliness
depriving you of your needs?
Have you ever cheated your expectation
Of being a knight on a steed?

Did life seem to numb,
Without a single beck or call?
Causing you to question
the purpose of it all?

Have you pondered about
A life without love?

213

Did you fester up inside
Like a wingless dove?

Did happiness once skin you?
Did regret reverb?
Did you lose the impression
Of your purpose to serve?

Did you desire peace
From somewhere inside?
Like a silent night
in wintertime?

Did you long for oceans
In their deep blue eyes?
Not considering the devastation
Of waves at high tide?

Did warmth forsake you
Through cold lies and distrust?
Did you ponder a desire that was hopeless,
But a "must"?

Still, I hope you find shelter
In not a house, but a home.
Remember, turbulance means
You're not traveling alone.

May 3
Day 149

What do I need?

Today, my professor asked us to reflect on how we will prepare for our final year of college. Instantly, my eyes span to my *Prentice*, *Starkey,* and other sports medicine textbooks. My mind fills with ideas as to how I plan to divide up its chapters, in order to annotate the texts cover-to-cover. While senior year is most notorious for the BOC exam, and the many tears and anxieties that will precede it, it also brings to light our transition into the "real" world. In just a few short months, we will all be applying for full time jobs, graduate assistantships, and graduate programs. We will be forced out of our comfort zones and into this new reality, whether we are ready or not. While it is vital for us to become proficient in our examination and evaluation skills, and have a firm understanding of the science behind our practice, there is so much to be learned about ourselves as learners, clinicians, and individuals.

If you asked me in September if I was going to be here, writing this paper, I would have laughed. I didn't think that there was a life beyond the starvation and depression I was plagued with. I thought that merely existing was all that was in the cards for me. I didn't believe that I served any purpose, other than that of self-destruction.

I hope to begin to develop a greater sense of bravery and purpose. Looking around, I have discovered that so many people settle, lackadaisically, for what is easy—they have settled for adequate jobs, adequate relationships, and adequate dreams. They wake up and discover that they have been living their lives out of convenience, and have lost the element of thrill and excitement that once sparked their lives with meaning.

On the contrary, each and every time an athlete steps onto the field, he/she risks it all. They are confident. They risk the possibility of injury or loss, in the sole hope that something amazing may happen. They play each game with the thrill and passion that I strive to embody every day.

In order to ultimately prepare for my senior year, I hope to not only learn more about my athlete's ailments and pathologies, but also about their bravery. Bravery is like a muscle—as we train it, it grows stronger and more powerful. Without utilization, it will atrophy, and its capacity to change our lives will be diminished.

Over my last three years in this program, I have been taught to not only anticipate the unexpected, but to welcome it with open arms. This year has definitely produced the unexpected. While I may have not initially given these happenings a warm welcome, I have learned to acknowledge, respect, and grow through my battles and obstacles.

As athletic trainers, we will be serving our patients. Be it a high school junior varsity football team, or the New York City Ballet Company, we assist them in tackling their obstacles. We are there to support them through those battles which are expected, and those which are not—whilst continuously encouraging them to pursue their dreams. These activities are often what give our patients a purpose. I hope to learn that this concept of "purpose" is not something that you magically discover one day. It is something that you must take risks to develop.

I hope to gain insight into the specific elements of this program, which give my life passion, meaning, and purpose. I hope to take more risks, without fear of being wrong. I refuse to graduate without an understanding of where I can facet my strengths to create meaning in this world. Even if that means changing the life of a just single athlete, discovering this insight will guide me in crafting my skillset.

May 4
Day 150

Marie's Philosophy.

We had been sitting in one of the group therapy rooms. I was curled up in the corner of the couch, staring at the clock. My eyes chased each ticking second, in hopes that maybe my glare would force time to go by quicker. I tuned out the ongoing conversation that surrounded me. It was something about shame, regret, or something else that I didn't want to face today. I just wasn't in the mood.

Suddenly, my ears tuned in to what might be the most ridiculous thing I have ever heard. There is this new client; she had just come back from residential. Her name is Marie. Anyway, I returned to the present just in time to hear her say "If I could go back and rewrite history… if I could go back and change my past, to prevent any of this from happening to me… I wouldn't."

My reaction wasn't nice. I actually feel really bad about it. After she spoke, I began to laugh. Uncontrollably. I didn't mean it. I wasn't mocking her. I guess I was just confused. "Who would ever wish this upon themselves again?" I curiously spoke up, "Why would you ever renew this hell upon yourself?"

Marie wasn't mad. She wasn't sad. She wasn't confused. She understood. She looked at me as if she was looking at her former self. She looked at me as if she knew exactly where I was coming from.

She took a deep breath in, and replied, "If I hadn't had to go through this… If I hadn't had to endure the challenges I came across every single day… If I didn't

218

learn how to fight for myself… I wouldn't be the same person that I am today".

I guess I never looked at it that way before.

And just
when the
caterpillar thought
her life was over
she began to
fly

May 6
Day 152

The Dream.

Last night I had a really weird dream. My eating disorder and I reunited. Except the ED took the image of a person. A man. *Ethan Dodds*. I could tell that it had been some time since we had last met. There was a tension, and it was awkward. We both had knowledge of our history—the good and the bad. He and I spotted each other across the shopping mall. I remember that the eye contact was as piercing as a sword.

As we went outside, you could see an open sky. No skyscrapers, no telephone poles or wires, no birds, no clouds, no light pollution. It was night time, and the stars were racing past us, as if time was lapsing without the return of day. He pointed out the pictures that the stars had formed, and connected the lines of the constellations. That was, until we came across a group of stars that seemed to spell out my name. For some reason, he tried and tried, but couldn't force those dots to align. It wasn't until I raised my hand, and pointed to the twinkling lights, that my signature became legible in the night sky.

May 7
Day 153

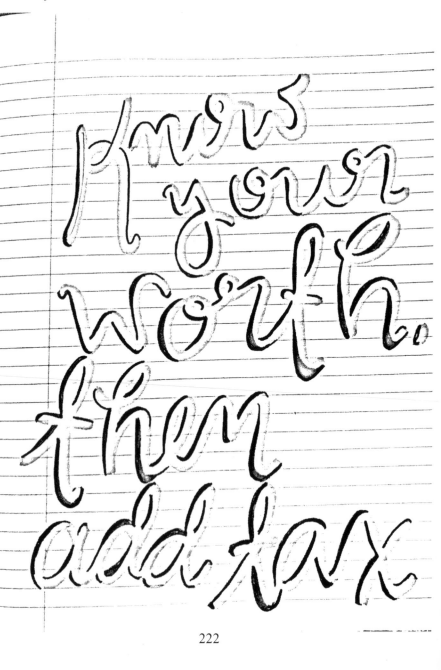

Just when you think you've been buried you've been planted

May 9
Day 155

May 10
Day 156

Day 17 (continued).

Today, I feel like a sheet of paper. Blank. Flimsy. As though the wind could blow, and I'd forever be lost. As though one wrong move, and I'll give someone a papercut. I am wrinkled. I'm trying, so desperately, to unfold myself. I'm impressionable to the slightest marking and scuff. I feel disposable.

But paper is also a pallet for endless possibilities. Today, I can write my love story, or my American dream, or I can simply start my pen for the adventures of tomorrow.

Hope came along with scissors—eager to snip away the damages. Hope left me anew. When I was unable to recognize myself, Hope guided my corners to each other. I found myself being able to connect parts of myself which seemed so far away. Hope taught me that I wasn't as fragile as I thought I was. Even ducks can turn into swans.

May 11
Day 157

I did it. I don't know how I did it. I'm free.

I'm moving out of my apartment in two days. The semester is over. I made it, but I'm still chained down by this stupid disorder. Today, in one of the group therapy sessions, I spoke about how one behavior, that I still can't manage to break, is weighing myself. Knowing my gravitational pull to the ground provides me with so much contentment. Knowing that I'm gaining weight in the way that *I* want to, instead of a way that I am oblivious to… it's just the single ounce of control that I still have in my life. I told the other clients that I knew that my parents were coming to help me move out. I knew that they would see the scale. They still thought that my therapist had my scale. You know, the one that she took back in January and that I replaced within the week. I knew that my parents would make me throw away my scale. I didn't want to do something, just because I was forced to do it. I want control. So, I chose to part with it on my own terms. I asked the other clients about what they thought I should do. Should I drop it down the stairs? Should I burn it? Should I run over it with my car?

Amelia told me about how she's disposed of her old, "sick" clothes. She found the thickest marker that she could find, and defaced the denim that once confined her. Then, she took a pair of scissors. She destroyed the pants the way that her eating disorder had destroyed her: she left them in pieces.

I liked that idea. I drove home quickly after treatment at TFC. I made a beeline for my office. I picked up all the paint and markers that I could fit into my hands, and dropped it off at the picnic table outside of my apartment. Then I went to my room and picked up the scale that sat in front of my full-length mirror. Without greeting my roommates, I walked with passion back outside. I sat at the table and slashed paint, unapologetically, across the glass that meant far too much to me. For, it is just a piece of metal. The paintbrush smeared the tears that rolled down my face, and onto the glass. I let the paint dry, and then grabbed the thick, black marker. Mindlessly, I jotted down every horrible adjective that I associated with myself. My hand moved quicker than my mind could process. I pressed hard against the glass until my knuckles were white, until my fingers were stained with ink, and until the scale held no more room for insecurity.

I capped the marker, and thought to myself, "Now what?" I knew that this wasn't enough. I needed to permanently separate myself from this monster. I needed to break it.

I carried the scale up a hill, adjacent to my apartment. My hands shook, as the weight of what I was about to do was much heavier than this 3lbs scale. When I made it to the top of the hill, I looked down. I remembered the first week of school. I remembered climbing up this hill for the first time, to get to class. I remembered the feeling of my legs giving out from under me. I remembered feeling weak.

"I am not weak", I whispered under my breath. I closed my eyes tightly. I felt my face getting hot. I felt the tears begin to cascade down my cheeks. And with that, I threw the scale on the floor.

And guess what.

It didn't break.

I started laughing. You have got to be kidding me, right? I picked the scale back up and saw that the battery had fallen out. I would have to do this again. I would have to build up the courage to do this again. I couldn't. I needed help. I called nearly everyone in my contacts list. Well, I mean I called those who I thought wouldn't judge me... those who have supported me from the beginning. No one was around. Classes were still in session, and dance practices were being held, and there was a big concert going on in New York or New Haven or some other "New-Something" City. I would have to do this alone.

Puddles of tears fell down my cheeks and hit the floor as I realized that, once again, I was alone. Except, this time, I wasn't going to look to anorexia as a crutch. I would not look to behaviors for solace. I would not buttress myself with restriction and continued isolation. This was it. At this moment, it was something that I had to do alone.

I took a deep breath, and choked back the last of the tears I would allow myself to cry over this disorder. I raised the scale far above my head, and, with all my might, threw it down the hill that once overtook me.

Glass fell down the slope. The destructive words shattered until they were illegible. I now saw the scale for what it was... it holds no significant essence of power. It's glass. It's just as fragile as *you* are. Except, this time, there's no one to patch its pieces together.

May 12
Day 159

My 95ᵗʰ Birthday

On my 95th birthday, I would like my grandmother to toast me. I would like her to talk about how far she has seen me grow over the years—from my playful childhood years to my angsty-teenaged phase. I hope she embellishes on how these years of early-adulthood struggles have shaped me into a fearless woman. I hope she tells me that I've lived a fierce life—a life that you look back on, and find leaving you breathless. The kind of life that you can picture in cinema and in literature. While I may not write the next great American novel, or successfully climb Mt. Everest, I hope that she can turn to be on my 95th birthday, and tell me that it was all worth it. For, after 95 trips around the sun, I found happiness.

May 13
Day 159

Life expands and contracts in proportion to our bravery

231

May 14
Day 160

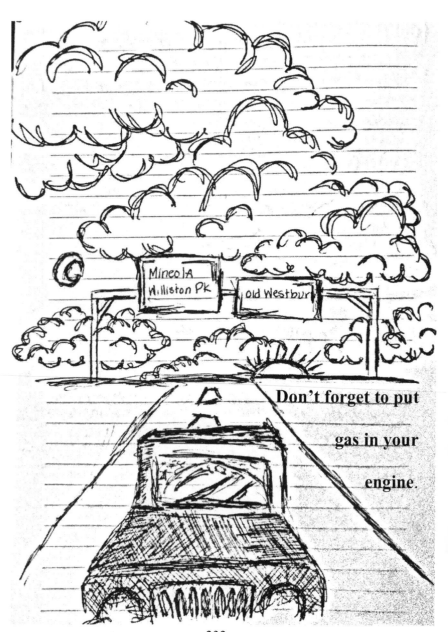

May 15
Day 161

Sailing.

> The devil plays his silly song
> As winds start to blow.
> Sailboats shake as we search along
> For a path, down to go.
> Thunder whispers quietly,
> As thoughts roar through our minds.
> Our faults begin to shower down,
> And pour on us like dimes.
>
> As a million raindrops
> Fell upon our heads,
> We swam upstream, against our tears,
> And made it to the bend.
> We cast a sail from broken dreams,
> And trek the earth and back.
> Lightning strikes, and thunder blows,
> And stops us in our tracks.
>
> Lights flicker on and off
> In this hell that we call home.
> Darkness engulfs all of those
> Who decide to stand alone.
> We've lost sight of our northern star.
> We begin to wonder and dream:
> If no one sees, or hears our screams,
> Will we even bleed?

May 16
Day 162

Why do I spend
my longing days
In hopes of preventing
tomorrow's rain?

What does my opinion
Hold and maintain?
What does it carry?
Or try to sustain?

Mindless chatter
hasn't a way
Of creating the miracle
Of a warm summer day.

I know I'll never
Stop a storm
Or end a summer
drought.

You can't expect
A garden to grow
When it's planted
In self-doubt.

May 17
Day 163

Rose's.

Today, my outpatient therapist and I planned on tackling a fear food—burgers. I want to discharge from TFC soon. I will not turn 21 there. I won't. I've been maintaining my weight since March. So, the one of the last steps, towards beating this monster, is making peace with food.

So, I drove up to her house after class. I walked up her cobblestone steps. Her poodle greeted me at the door, as he did each week. Rose guided me to her backyard. On the deck was a long glass table. She had set the table with beautiful china. Placemats were lined with far too many pieces of silverware, and elegant wine glasses were filled to the brim with *Ensure*. All this, just to eat a burger.

Her home is nestled high on a hill. It's modeled after the "American Dream"—a wrap-around porch, blue shutters, a white picket fence, a red door. I remember the first time I had come to her home.

After the fiasco with the first counseling appointment, I was done with mental health professionals. I was over it. "You don't need anyone but yourself," my disorder echoed. The sense of paranoia I had, revolving around other's opinions of me, had magnified. In a world of 7+ billion people, I was alone.

I had never gone to a therapist before. My brother had, and a few of my friends had, but something about it didn't sit well with me. Maybe it was the fact that

I believed that I should be able to solve all of my problems on my own. Maybe it was the fact that I didn't want to burden another with the weighted grief I carried inside. Maybe I was scared to let someone in.

My mom and godmother found Rose through Google. The way that they described the website made me think of *Match.com,* except for those who need 45-60 minutes of tear-soaked couch time. Actually, now thinking about it, is that much different than finding a significant other?

Anyway, my mom called Rose to make an appointment for me. My mom was scared that I wouldn't call. Smart woman. The voice that met my mothers on the other end of the line was strong. It was direct and clear. The moment of intimidation, that my mom had experienced during the call, made her confident. Maybe, just maybe, this is what I needed.

Meanwhile, I was at school. In between classes, I would go outside. The warm September heat blanketed my everlasting goosebumps. I would sit outside of the lecture hall, near the fountain. I'd allow the sun to embrace my face as I simultaneously embraced my body—in hopes that the compression would ease the aches and pains I felt.

My mother called me to tell me that my appointment would be the following Tuesday. Defensively, I reiterated that I had a handle on my life. That I didn't need external help. That I had control. She fell silent and told me that, if I ditched the appointment, she'd pull me out of school. "Perfect daughters don't get kicked out of school", I thought. So, I apprehensively and unenthusiastically showed up on that rainy Tuesday.

Our first sessions weren't pretty. I sat across from her, on a soft love-seat, which I too greatly wished would consume me. I clenched on to the throw pillows and held them over my stomach, desperate to hide. I wasn't an ideal client, to say the least. Our first sessions maintained a consistency of two moods: that of silence and one-word answers, or a flash-flood of sobs. My mood varied as black-and-whitely as I lived my life. Rose was kind, though. She was gentle and compassionate. She was patient. I began seeing Rose 2-3 times per week.

Slowly, Rose began to chip away at the walls that I ever-so-cautiously built up. I began to unravel. I began to discover who I was, behind the mountains of plastered ideals. But, in spite of her best efforts, I continued to drop weight. I was plummeting further and further down a path of self-destruction. While I was making progress along the road of understanding myself and recognizing my emotions, I still couldn't find rationale in ending the era of abuse and harm.

On a cold November afternoon, Rose told me that she would no longer see me if I didn't begin a higher level of treatment. I begged Rose to let me stay with her. I promised her that I would put on weight. I promised her that I would comply with my meals and medications. I promised her that I would try. She was unwavering. Without a word, she handed me a business card. It contained the contact information for The Flourish Collaborative's admissions department. With tear-filled eyes, I reached out and accepted the card.

And I'm lucky that I did. Rose saved my life.

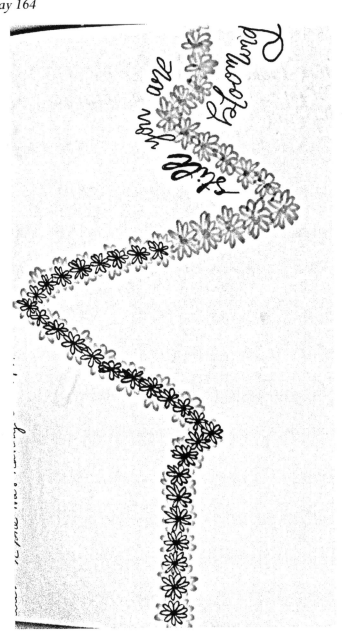

May 19

Day 165

Rising.

       So often we try
       To live like a star.
       Leaving everyone warm,
       No matter how far.

       Shining for hours on end
       To light up the dark,
       From desolate streets,
       To community parks.

       But at some point, the sun
       Must say its goodbyes,
       And allow the moon
       To rise in the sky.

       For, even when the day
       Fades into the night,
       The moon is still there
       To provide ample light.

       Illuminating the road
       So dull, dark, and gray
       To guide you home
       Each step of the way.

       Even without
       The warmth and the heat,

The night provides gleam
When life screams defeat.

So even when life
Seems anything but bright,
Always remember
There's hope in the night.

May 20
Day 166

Our Books.

For as long as I can remember, I have looked to books for solace. When I've found myself unable to cope, I've found peace in poetry. When I've found myself hopeless, I've found positivity in self-help manuals. When I've found myself curious, I delve into texts on architecture and design. Truly, I owe a large portion of the person I am today to the books I have read in the past. The characters in my favorite books have often taught me more than my high school professors have. From watching my favorite characters recuperate from heartbreak, to joyfully cheering them on through their victories, reading has provided me with a life-skill at an early age. I guess this skill is empathy.

C.S. Lewis said something like, "Literary experience heals the wound, without undermining the privilege, of individuality". Reading provides you with anecdotal experiences of others. It allows one's brain to interpret experiences, which one may have yet to encounter. It provides the reader with someone to relate to, or a lesson, which may soothe a damaged soul. No two encounters or experiences are the same, as each individual interprets them differently. Literature allows one to take a front-row seat into the most private thoughts of the characters.

In life, it is very easy to be selfish and self-centered. If you think about it, you have only ever truly known one side of the story—your own. Without inquiry, it is impossible to know what others are thinking, and how they are interpreting different chains of events. It can be difficult to develop characteristics of empathy and compassion for others without social, real-life experience. Books allow you to experience moments that may not present themselves in your life, but that may provide you with extraordinary lessons on understanding others. Truly, individuals who shut out literature are missing out on the splendor of perspective. Seeing the world through the eyes of another is an experience that cannot otherwise be had.

I used to get really upset when people wouldn't ask me questions about what I was going through. I felt like they didn't care. Maybe, they didn't want to know about the dialogue that was killing me. I didn't know. Now I am starting to wonder if people just didn't know what questions to ask. How are you supposed to relate to another when you have no idea what is going on in their minds?

I think I'm gonna share some of these entries with people. Maybe people will want to understand.

May 21
Day 167

Whenever you feel like giving up, remember:

- Do it to get your smile back.
- Do it to get your happiness back.
- Do it to, once again, find radiance in each day.

May 22
Day 168

Things I'm Grateful For:

3. My roommates' friendship and bonds
4. Late night study sessions before exams, that make you more confident than dismal
5. Cups of tea. Ones that are hot, but just cool enough to not leave you with a burnt tongue
6. Uncontrollable laughter, that leaves your stomach hurting
7. People who still open the door open for me, even when I'm 1000 feet away
8. Spell check

May 23
Day 169

Love.

> I think I'm falling in love with the idea of falling in love
> with something other than my eating disorder.
> My heart burns for longing.
> It desires the understanding of something other than
> calorie counting and shrinking myself.
> Someone, please help me.
> I don't know what this is.
> Am I finally moving on from my break up
> with Ethan Dodds?

May 24
Day 170

The Bean

I used to sing at open mics. I used to love singing. Music has this funny way of drawing in solace. For those brief moments that you are captured by a song, the rest of the world melts away. It is just you, and the lyrics.

A few of my high school friends asked me if I wanted to sing with them tonight. There's this coffee shop that has open mic nights each Thursday. I used to perform at them all of the time. But today, I really didn't want to. The thought of putting myself out there... to have dozens of eyes pinned onto me... I imagine that they would sting like a thousand mosquito bites. I spent so much time trying to hide... maybe this would be too much? But, something inside of me found nostalgia in the idea. So, I agreed. After treatment, I drove down to the coffee shop.

I put on a dress, some heels, and wore my favorite lipstick. Maybe if I pretended that things were the way that they used to be...they *would* be. And you know what? I had so much fun! I got to sing again. I got to experience the breath-of-fresh-air that a perfectly pitched B minor provides you with. I got to, once again, do something that makes me happy. That's what this is all about.

When I have a really hard time with accepting the weight-gain, I think back to moments like these. Moments when I experience *true* happiness. *These* moments are what make recovery worth it. For those brief moments that you are captured by a song. For those moments that you lose sight of the rest of the world. For those moments when all else fades away. For finding your smile again. For finding joy again. For finding ease again.

247

That's what this is all about. This is what makes it worth it.

When the night was over, one of the other performers walked me to my car. I didn't catch his name. I couldn't even guess what it could have been. He's definitely not a "Mitch", and definitely not a "Charlie". I don't know. Let's call him *the Guy*. So, on the chilly walk back to the parking lot, *the Guy* and I spoke about our favorite sets of the night. I greeted him "goodbye" as I opened my car door. "Wait," he interrupted, "I have a question".

"There's this moment," he continued, "between lyrics, and between verses, when you're not singing. During those moments, you wear this smile…like you're nervous or insecure. And I was just wondering… why? Why are you so insecure?"

Well, that's intrusive. Like, geez. When was the last time a stranger said to you: "Hi. I'm new in town, and I'd like to know the backbone of your deepest, most innate insecurities". But, hey. I'd probably never see him again. Why not be anything but honest? "Well," I answered, "I am incredibly self-conscious."

He took a step back and looked at me with curious eyes. He answered, calmly, "Well, you have no reason to be".

May 25
Day 171

Breathe.

You deserve to nourish your body.
You deserve it.
I deserve it.

Would you tell your sister not to eat her lunch?
No.
Would you be okay with your brother skipping dinner?
No.
Would you compliment your best friend on her growling stomach?
No.

Why, then, is it okay for you to restrict yourself?

You finally have your happiness back. Isn't that wonderful?

Maybe someone will fall in love with you.
Maybe that someone will be yourself.

May 26
Day 172

The Beach.

Kat and I went to the beach today. It was the first time I had been in a bathing suit in over a year. I was so self-conscious when I was getting ready. I thought of every reason not to eat while I was with her. I couldn't stand the thought of perpetuating the expansion and bloat that I feared would scare my friend away. What could I tell her? That I already ate breakfast, and lunch, and dinner before 10 am? That, in spite of the 95° weather, I still insisted on wearing my baggy pants and a hooded sweatshirt, in hopes of hiding my body under the heaps of fabric? Maybe if I just lay in the sun, people won't see the contours, and cellulite, and my perceived imperfections. Summer is supposed to be fun. Beach trips are supposed to be fun. It's supposed to be a season of embracing the Vitamin D and daydreaming 24/7. It is supposed to be an escape from the stresses of academia. When did the disconnect occur? When did we become more concerned with the shape of our bodies, as opposed to the build of our sandcastles?

I ended up deleting the Instagram app off of my phone because there were way too many bikini selfies circulating. It just fed into my negative body image, and poor self-esteem. I spent some time comparing myself to others I saw. Seeing how beautiful, and confident, and happy those pictures were. I began picking myself apart— piece-by-piece—like a sculptor and a mallet.

I thought about it some more, and I stopped myself. What was I doing? Why was I allowing myself to fall down this rabbit hole? Why am I inflicting this pain on myself? I don't have to do this to myself.

They always say that social media is a huge contributor to crippling self-esteem issues. I always thought that was a bit silly. "I can control how I allow these images to make me feel", I'd say. "These images cannot have power over me if I don't allow them to".

I've recently learned that you can't control your thoughts. They come in like waves. You never know how devastating, or how gentle, they will crash. All you can do is control your actions, following the thought. You can allow yourself to run away and hide from the water, or you can plant your feet in the sands of self-assurance, and know that the wave will pass.

I think I'm going to take a bit of a break from social media, now.

May 27
Day 173

The MET

I went into the city today. I decided to go the the Metropolitan Museum of Art, my favorite place in the world. It's weird, but I feel like a haunting peace has fallen over me. As I walked through Central Park, in all its eerie silence, I wondered if I would ever have a moment of peace from my own intrusive thoughts.

Even in that quiet park, melodic voices rang throughout my ears. Ideas formed. To-Do's listed. Thoughts of self-destruction and deprivation rang louder and louder.

But, once I stepped into the museum, the voices silenced and I felt like I could breathe again. It was at that moment that I understood what it means to find *my place*. I guess because this place is so sacred to me, my mind found that it should be treated as such, and be respectful.

Miraculously, I found a pen on the floor, after scrambling for one in my purse for minutes on end. I needed to jot this down. I think this moment was meant for me to experience. Maybe my body could become *my place* if I treated it like the sacred space it is.

May 28
Day 174

The Barbeque

Ready for a laugh? So, I had so much fun at the beach with Kat the other day. It was a perfect day. Well, except for one thing. Somewhere between the reminiscent conversation, and the laughter, I forgot to apply sunscreen.

I am so sunburnt. I have never experienced anything like this before. I always thought that my internal turmoil burned. Wow. I had *no* idea. Every inch of my body, every wrinkle on my face, each aspect of my being was covered in blisters and burns. I look like a literal monster. I used to always be so self-conscious of others seeing my perceived imperfections. Now, I *know* that people are staring at me. I *know* that they are judging me. I thought that these stares were similar to the way people looked at me when I was emaciated.

It was interesting. I went to see Rose this morning. When she answered the door, a look of concern draped her eyes. She was compassionate and empathetic to my sun-poisoned aesthetic. There was no judgment. There was no laughter. There was just concern. Maybe this is how people felt when I was deep into my disorder. Maybe people weren't judging me because they thought I was fat, or ugly, or a loser. Maybe those silent stares were actually cries of concern.

After my appointment with Rose, my family and I drove down to Maryland for our annual Memorial Day Family BBQ. I have been dreading this party for weeks.

You see, at my sickest. I really didn't have much support from anyone, other than my parents, my best friend, Sara, and Rose. No concerned inquiries, no calls, no texts. There was no conversation. My mom would tell me that *Joe Shmoe*, and *Sally Snowflake*, would ask about me. They would send her messages of well-wishes. My mom would tell me about how loved and supported I was by our family. But, I was always curious as to why those individuals never directly reached out to me. It made me believe that my mom was lying to me. It made me believe that everyone hated me for being sick. It made me believe that this was my fault. It made me believe that this was a choice that *I* made. It made me feel alone. I realize now that, most likely, their silence towards me was centered around fear—fear of what they'd say, fear that they'd trigger me, fear that I'd get worse, fear of what my answers may actually be. However, I'll never truly know what their rationale behind that was. It hurt. It broke me.

Since then, things haven't been the same with my friendships or familial relationships. "Maybe they 'abandoned' you, because they thought that their lives would be easier without you," I thought, "they didn't sign up to take care of the sick friend/niece/cousin". But, oh boy, did I shut down that distortion quickly.

On the four-hour drive down the east coast, and in between reapplying layers of aloe vera, I daydreamed. I thought about the support I *did* have. I thought about the love I *have* received. I thought about the love that I *still* receive. If I spend my life sulking on those things which I don't have, I will lose sight of the gloriousness of today. If my family members decide to use this gathering as an

254

opportunity to isolate me because of my blistered skin, or extra pounds, then those individuals aren't my true family. Family is there to provide you with compassion, love, and empathy in the way that they know how.

Even if that way is silence, I know that a family without love is simply not a reality I will dwell in.

May 29
Day 175

The Car.

Where can your body take you on a full tank of gas? What parts do you need to get serviced and monitored? What would happen if you didn't get an oil change? Or check the breaks? Or care for the tires? What if you let your battery run out? What if you forgot where to find a service station? What if I'm stranded alone in some forgotten wasteland without AAA? What would happen if I couldn't afford gas?

Well, part of me wants to say that this vehicle is transient. Who cares if it crashes and burns? It's just an object. It is just a collection of metal. It's just a coalition of gears and trinkets. Who cares?

Well, what about the person that built it? The person who spend grueling hours on their hands and knees. Someone, somewhere, put their heart and soul into building this machine.

Well, I think I need to be the one to care. This vehicle needs to serve as a vessel. It must carefully and safely transport its passengers. If the care is crashed, but still runs, how is that beautiful?

You see, it doesn't matter if you have a Buick or a BMW. It doesn't matter if you have a Mercedes or a minivan. A car that is shining, and recieves regular repairs and lots of care... that's a beautiful car. Beauty comes from being managed with kindness—from the inside, out—free from chip dust and cigarette smoke.

256

May 30

Today, I decided to be happy.
Not only because it is good
For my mental and physical health,
But because we are all given
A limited amount of time on this Earth.
I refuse to spend another moment wasting it.
I refuse to be preoccupied with wishing
I said "I love you",
Or cautiously weighing my grams of lettuce.
I will no longer allow the way
In which others perceive me
To limit the way I choose to explore my life.
I will do what makes me happy.
I will imagine those who find fault in these ways
To be specks of dirt on my windshield.
I will remember that dirt
Can be easily washed away.

May 31
Day 177

Things I'm Grateful For:

1. To have eyes that can see the stars
2. To have ears that can hear the birds chirp
3. To have a nose that can smell sunflowers
4. To have the imagination to dream
5. To have an abundance of energy to pursue my desires
6. To have the capacity to love and be loved
7. To have the hope to make it to tomorrow

JUNE
BLOOMING

June 1
Day 178

Memories.

Today, I thought about why I am so afraid of gaining weight. The thing is, I can't remember where it started...

There are points where I find myself stopping in time. I take a moment to mentally capture the sights I see, the aromas I smell, the sounds I hear. Sometimes I find myself praying that I'll remember those moments forever. But, it's all about the smallest, most minoscule moments. It's those most seemingly mundane moments which shape us into the people that we are today.

They say that each time you recall a memory, it changes a bit in your mind. Maybe this is why we find it difficult to recall the origins of our most innate fears. Maybe your mind wants to keep these life-altering occurrences in their purest, most natural form. Maybe in doing so, those moments are erased from our memories and, instead, imprinted on the soul.

June 2
Day 179

Progress.

With winter,
Comes spring.

With crappy,
Comes happy.

With rain,
Comes flowers.

With darkness,
Comes light.

With failure,
Comes learning.

With help,
Comes hope.

With sadness,
Comes joy.

June 3

Day 180

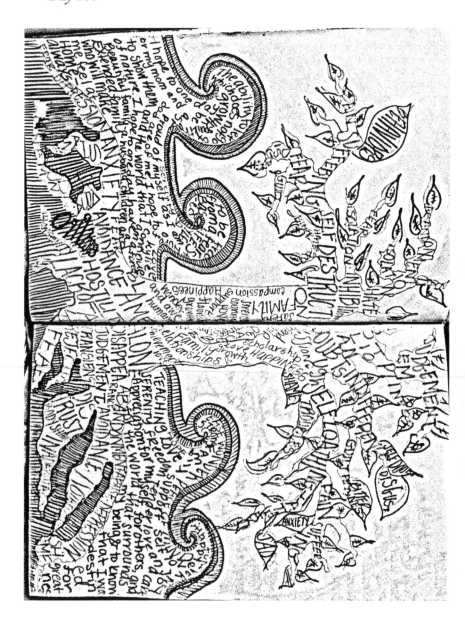

June 4
Day 181

Change.

It's the feeling of the air
As it begins to change.
My thoughts have turned,
Recognizing the miracle of age.

Change surrounds us.
Each sun brings a new day,
Like how the blossoms spring up
Each and every May.

The air turns cold
As suns begin to set.
Change is all around us.
It is a choice that we let

Stay open, and hopeful,
And accepting to be
A miraculous splendor
Of a life never seen.

Sometimes though,
Frustration sticks.
It ties us down
Like shackles and bricks.

Hope starts to fade,
Like dusk at the sea.

We come up with a million
Reasons to leave.

Hope becomes lost
In a sea of mistakes.
The "what ifs" crash.
Each wave makes us break.

But leaves change color
And fall to the ground.
No one questions their changes.
No one makes a sound.

The world knows that leaves
Can change, and they will.
But why assume that people
Cannot fit that same bill?

Through the coldest of winters,
And the hottest of Junes,
The miracle of change
Hums to its own tune.

Change follows no path.
It leads its own way.
It flows through each week,
Each season, each day.

June 5
Day 182

"Dwell in Possibility"

"Dwell in Possibility" is a quote by Emily Dickenson. I want to begin to run with this quote. I want this quote to shape my life, as well as all of my pursuits. I think…well, I mean, I hope that I will not only dwell on the possibility of absolutely every opportunity, but God, I hope I flourish in each, as well. There is kindness in every moment, and always something to be grateful for.

A few weeks ago, I laughed when Marie told me that she would never rewrite her history. I didn't get it. I didn't understand what good could possibly come out of a journey like this. I think I'm starting to understand it now.

The inner demons, that scream into my ears, taught me that you cannot believe everything you hear.

The distorted image I see in the mirror has taught me that you cannot judge a book by its cover. Not everything is truly as it seems.

It is important to know that sometimes, things don't unfold as they are expected to. But, life has a funny way of working out. In the meantime, it's important to allow yourself to cry, and to feel emotions. Are there days I'd love to forget? Sure! Are there memories that still haunt me? Of course! But, these moments have shaped me into who I am today, and, regardless of where you are on your journey, it is important to accept yourself — each feeling, each inch, each moment. Perseverance is perhaps the greatest strength of all. You see, recovery isn't linear. I used to beat myself up all the time. Either, I wasn't the "perfect anorexic", or I wasn't the "perfect recoverer". And it wasn't until I surrendered the fight for this inconceivable perfection that I was able to find who I truly am. I an not "the anorexic". I am not "the recoverer". I am not "the perfection". I am *me. Me.* And, wow. How beautiful it is to be my own.

June 6
Day 183

The Realization.

And then, it happens. One day you'll wake up and your first thought won't be about how much you hate yourself. Or the fact that you slept on your stomach and now your hip bones are bruised. Or that you don't know if you'll be able to stand to live one more day in this body. One day you'll wake up and get out of bed. You'll shut off your alarm and tidy up your sheets. You'll walk into the bathroom, brush your teeth, and you'll head into the kitchen to put a K Cup in the Keurig. You'll carry on with your morning, and head to class. And it won't be until sitting in that lecture for 35 minutes that you realized you didn't weigh yourself that morning. You'll realize that you didn't kick yourself for not weighing out your oatmeal, or measuring out the ounces of coffee creamer. You'll be sitting in those stiff desk chairs and not feel the pain of the firm plastic backs against your exposed spine. You'll realize that you weren't out of breath after climbing up that hill, outside of your apartment. You'll realize that you didn't feel like you wanted to die today.

Recovering from an eating disorder is not about waking up one morning and falling in love with every inch of this body that you were gifted with. It's not about learning to intuitively eat, or to never have a shameful thought again. Recovery comes with finding peace and solace in life's discomforts.

June 7
Day 184

Things I'm Grateful For:

1. People who won't hide things from you in order to prevent you from being mad or upset.
2. Conquering a really difficult fouette combination.
3. The moment when you realize that a certain song is no longer stuck in your head.
4. Nights where you have no trouble falling asleep.
5. 2 for $20 candle sales.
6. Freedom and independence.
7. The smell of coffee.
8. The first stretch of the morning.
9. When you arrive to a movie just late enough to miss the pre-screen trivia games, but just in time to catch the trailers.
10. Those nights where you can fall asleep knowing that you did the best you possibly could. You faced every moment with strength, and applied yourself.

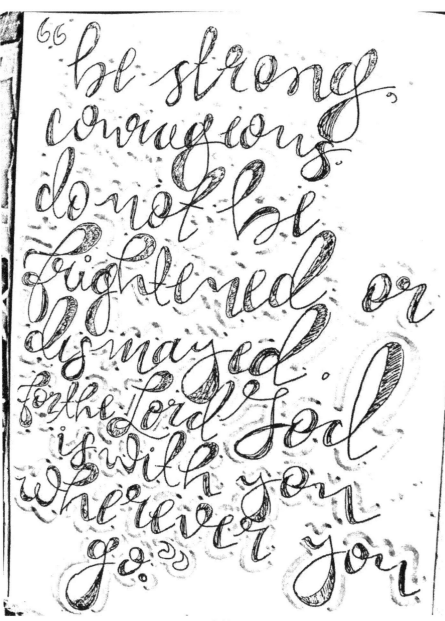

"be strong, courageous. do not be frightened or dismayed. for the Lord God is with you wherever you go."

June 9
Day 186

Pride.

Each day, I can scream and shout about the importance of self-love and body-acceptance. I can fill social media feeds with my endless collection of positive affirmations. I can articulate all of the work I've put in towards accepting my body, my mind, and my spirit. I can reminisce about the process of finding peace within myself. I can vent about the topics of diet culture and societal expectations.

But that's not the point.

Look in the mirror. What do you see? You see *you*. All of *you*—complete with your flaws and your insecurities. You may see someone who didn't get enough sleep the night before. Perhaps you see someone who looks great in those new jeans. Maybe you simply just see your image, questioning how someone could possibly have the time and desire to look deeper than that.

Despite it all, you are able to carry on with your day. You are able to move past that blemish or scar, tossing it to the side as just a pointless nothing. Sure, it may cause a blow to your self-esteem, but it's nothing you can't handle.

You are resilient.

I've talked about this countless times before, but when I look in the mirror, I do not see myself. I see my eating disorder. I see shame. I see a monster that has inhabited the home of my spirit.

Whilst never really as successful as I wish to be, each moment presents itself as a new opportunity to recover. Each glance, which I abstain from self-deprecation and behaviors, places me one step further on the path to self-acceptance and compassion.

I'm not sure if I will ever be 100% happy with myself, but I'm working on it each and every day.

And, for that, I am proud of myself.

June 10
Day 187

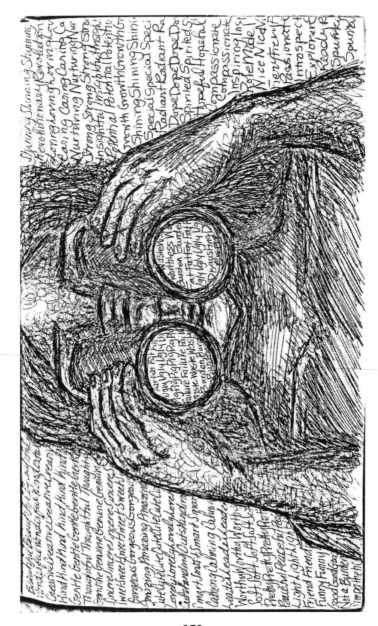

June 11

June 12
Day 189

A Life with Happiness.

It's easy to fall into the trap that life can be. We get consumed in a schedule; we say we're going to do something, then, before we know it, months have passed us by and we haven't made a single change. It can be so easy to fall victim to the routines of day-to-day life, allowing yourself to just fall into the rhythm of the tide.

They say that happiness is a choice. We have the power to pave our lives. Don't settle for it. "Choosing happiness" is not congruent with fulfilling a life that society deems acceptable.

Life has been kind enough to present you with a fresh start every morning. Each day is an opportunity. You can go anywhere in the world. You can do things you've only dreamed of. Don't miss out on it because you don't feel capable of it. You are. You're capable of anything. You were meant to accomplish the unimaginable in this lifetime. Purpose is not found in shrinking thyself, but instead in the ability to grow...to fall in love with each and every day of the rest of your life.

I've found that the fear of being alone, and the fear of failure, has led me to a dead-end life. This path has led me to unhappiness. I've silenced my inner being, in hopes to comply with unrealistic expectations. If you always fear failure, you will never accomplish anything great. Relinquishing oneself from the fear of the unknown... Escaping the fear of physical, mental, and intellectual growth… that is the first step to changing the world. It is the first step in living fiercely, ferociously, and passionately on a path you choose. Don't allow life to pass you by, due to hesitation.

Whether you're 7 or 97, it's never too late to chase your goals, and to wake up to do something you love every day. And most importantly, don't settle because it's easy, or because it's comfortable. From here on out, I hope that you may all find the courage to fully participate in life. To shed kindness upon this vessel which carries you along your journey. To love fearlessly. To never settle for less—less life, less love, less joy, less fulfillment.

Kirsten,

I believe your presence is one that is meant to be felt by others. It is too vibrant, too warm, it offers too much to not be shared with the world. First, you must nurture, nourish and love this light of yours before you can offer it to any worthy person before you. I hope you choose wisely who you share it with, always reserving the love, compassion for your soul that will keep that light glowing, because it is too special, too precious to be spread thin. It is exciting to watch you be brave and reap the benefits of this experience. I am grateful to have crossed paths with you along your journey + mine. You are brave, you are so beautiful. And you have so much depth in the worth of your existence that has yet to be explored by you. ♡

275

June 13
Day 191

Unwavering Thoughts

There may come times in your life when you fail
to see the beauty of your being. There may come times in
your life when you fail to see the grace of your spirit. Life
can overflow with shame, and regret, and words left
unsaid. The "what ifs" can echo as loud as alarms, on
nights as hollow as the feeling of loneliness. No matter
what, the empty thoughts roar as loud as ghosts that haunt
you at night. They scream, and they taunt, and they bully.
You fall victim to the barracks of your own psyche.
You're in a pit. You're digging yourself into a hole.

Your dreams rest on the uneasy balance board of
your fears, and just as quickly, you can fall. You can fall
down the rabbit hole of your soul into the abyss of a life
not lived. How marvelous is it that we can allow
ourselves to grasp and tinker with the distaste of subtlety.

Life is funny. I drove all the way from TFC to this
little coffee shop where we played a few weeks ago. Isn't
it funny how freeing it is to return to a place where no
one knows anything about you? They don't know your
past, or your insecurities. Hell, they probably don't even
know my name. They probably don't even know *your*
name.

June 14
Day 192

The Untethered Soul

The untethered soul
Is a marvelous thing.
To wander and venture
To places unseen.

Free from restriction,
And loathing, and scorn.
Only room for beauty,
And things to adorn.

The untethered soul
Must be extreme
To relinquish its demons
From the anchors upstream.

Free to wallow and swell
In a jubilant feast,
Some place where
The sun sets in the east.

The untethered soul
Must silently keep
Free from protrusions
That too often weep

About worries too big,
And dreams too small,

Making you wonder:
who wanted peace, after all?

The untethered soul
is a paradise within.
Its presence will sing
With the cellos and mandolins.

It'll play you a lullaby
Each and every time
You find yourself melting
From the heated fear inside.

So, honey don't you dare
Begin to cry.
There's enough rain that pours
From clouds in the sky.

I promise that each day,
A new sun will rise,
And spring will return
After winter's goodbye.

Thunder's tender call
Bellows to claim
That even beautiful flowers
Need a little rain.

Lightning will strike
And burn through the breeze
To remind you that light

Still shines, in the darkest scenes.

So sing, untethered soul,
Like the rustling leaves.
Tell the beautiful night
It's not as lonely as it seems.

June 15
Day 193

From this day forward, I agree to fully participate in life. I agree to shed kindness on this vessel, which carries me along this journey. For the duration of my time on Earth, I agree to continually strive for mental, emotional, and spiritual benefit. While I acknowledge that pain is inevitable, I agree to channel those emotions through avenues of self-growth, as opposed to self-destruction. I will not use my body to prove my pain.

I further agree to accept this body—which is imperfect and vulnerable. I accept that with time, comes the changing, aging, and decay of my body. I acknowledge that with these changes comes wisdom, understanding, strength, and memories. Therefore, I agree to live a life that is accepting—to myself and others. For, if we were expected to journey upon this road alone, God would not have provided us with friends, family, animals, or over 7 billion beautiful strangers who inhabit this world for the same fulfillment.

With this agreement, I relinquish my soul from the fear of the unknown. I relinquish my soul from the fear of physical, intellectual, emotional, and spiritual growth. I acknowledge that I am destined for greatness. I acknowledge that I am capable of the unimaginable.

I understand that my ultimate purpose in life is not to shrink myself. I agree to nourish and fuel my body. I will allow myself the energy to sustain a life which is deserving of happiness. I agree to never settle for less—less life, less love, less joy, less happiness, less fulfillment.

Today, I choose peace over compulsion. I choose relationships over isolation. I choose happiness over shame. I choose self-love over self-deprecation. I choose independence. I choose freedom.

I agree to love and appreciate my body for all of its God-given, unfathomable capacities. I acknowledge the resentment, the judgments, and the criticisms that my mind cries out. I acknowledge that these thoughts are disordered, and I will work endlessly to redirect them. I was given this body for a reason—not to get straight A's, or to be successful, or to be beautiful. I was given this body as a vehicle. I was given this body as a protector of my soul. I acknowledge that in order to love and respect my body, I must first learn to love and accept my inner being.

I agree to celebrate life, and not to diminish it. This is the beginning of my new life, my new outlook on the world. This is an open door to endless opportunity. I am capable of releasing my being from these chains that have confined me for so long. I will take a breath. I will look up and thank the stars. I will live presently in each moment. I will love. I will be loved.

Today, I discharged from TFC.
Today, I choose to live a full life.

ABOUT THE AUTHOR

KIRSTEN CUNHA is full-time student at Sacred Heart University, where she is pursuing a degree in Athletic Training. This is her first work. She hopes to utilize her experiences to make strides in improving the education, preception, and conversation surrounding mental illness in athletic populations. She resides, with her loving parents, brother, and sister, in Mineola, New York.